MW01093255

# BOBBITO'S

# BOOK OF

# B-BALL

# BONG

# BONG!

## A MEMOIR OF SPORTS | STYLE | SOUL

EDGE

OF SPORTS

All rights reserved. No part of this book may be reproduced, stored in a retrieval system, or transmitted in any form, by any means, including mechanical, electronic, photocopying, recording, or otherwise, without the prior written consent of the publisher.

Published by Akashic Books
©2025 Bobbito García
Designer: Andrés Jiménez/@sieteson
Front cover photo: David "Dee" Delgado
Photography/Illustrations/Lettering (unless otherwise credited): Bobbito García

ISBN: 978-1-63614-230-2
Library of Congress Control Number: 2024949340

First printing
Printed in China

Edge of Sports
c/o Akashic Books
Instagram, X, Facebook: AkashicBooks
info@akashicbooks.com
www.akashicbooks.com

# DEDICATION

**This book is dedicated to . . .**

those who have crashed against poles, chain-link fences, and asphalt after taking it to the butter, and have gotten up and kept playing;

those who have scraped open their palms after falling from trying to cook their defender with some freak disco;

those who have sweated in the sun so much in one day that their faces were crusted with dried salt;

those who have played outdoors so many years they can put their hands on top of their kneecaps and feel their bones chiseling against each other;

those who have felt the sting of acid from peeling an orange because their fingertips have open wounds from clapping boards too much;

those who have never had a tan below their sock line because they don't know what it is to be outdoors and not be playing ball;

those who have played with leather balls outdoors until they became suede and light enough to be taken off by a summer breeze;

those who have played on double rims, low rims, biddy rims, bent rims, hanging-for-dear-life-on-one-remaining-bolt rims;

those who didn't have rims, who have shot on the bottom step of a fire-escape ladder, bottomless milk crate, or empty trash can;

those who can play high school or college for four years;

those who go pro and may stay at that level for a decade, if lucky;

most importantly, those who lovingly dedicate themselves to playground basketball . . . for life.

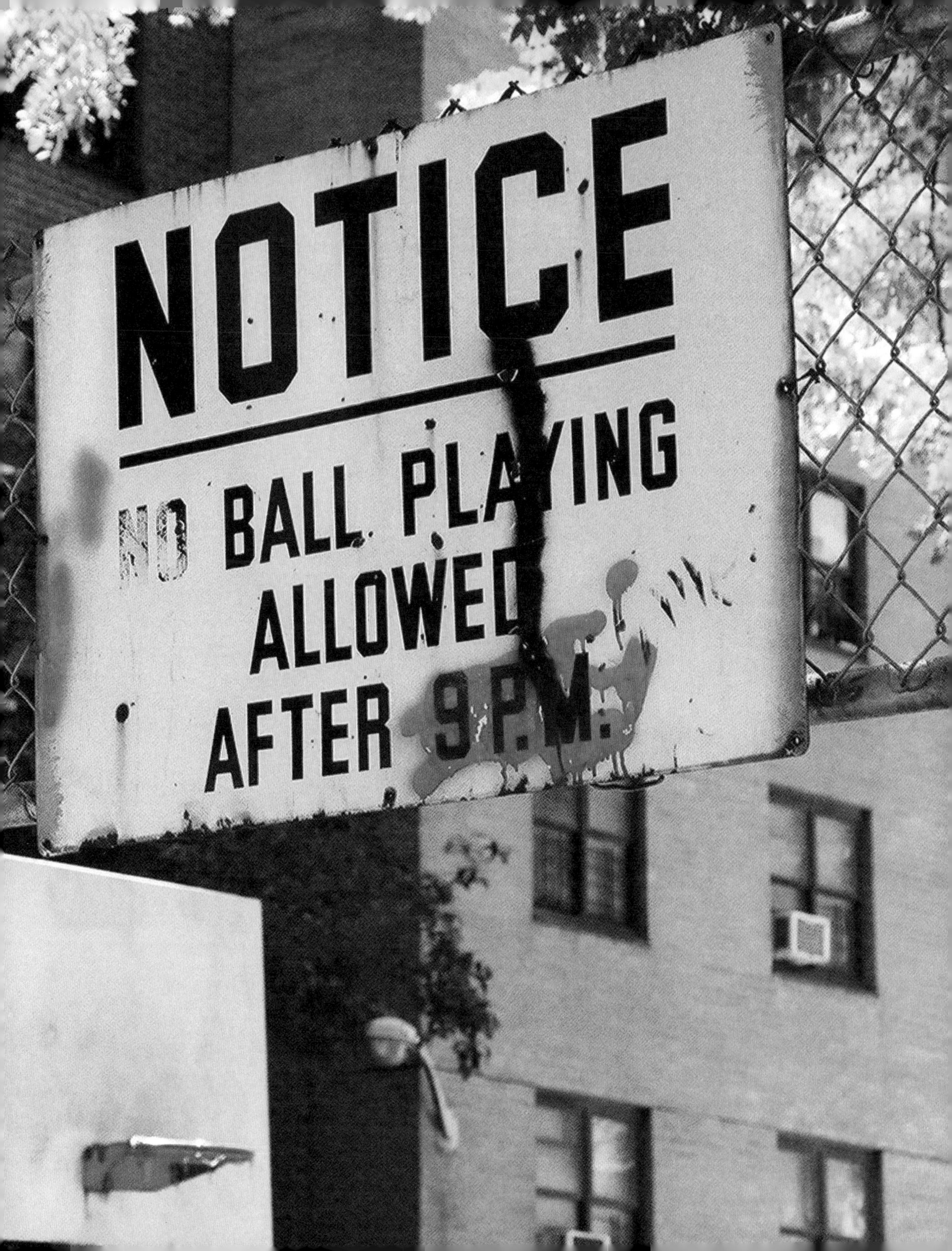
NOTICE
NO BALL PLAYING
ALLOWED
AFTER 9 P.M.

# CONTENTS

# The
# Happy
# Burger
# Days

# "Bobby, change the channel. *Now.* The Knicks are playing."

"But Daddy, *Happy Days* is about to start, and then at eight thirty *Welcome Back, Kotter* comes on!"

This was the usual exchange on a Tuesday night at our crib in the midseventies, and of course I always took an L. My father, Ramón García, was a huge Knicks fan and with good cause. They had won the NBA chip in 1970 and '73. Dad once had drinks with the squad's all-star guards Earl Monroe and Walt "Clyde" Frazier, two of the coolest celebrities one could meet in the Big Apple (with no apologies to '69 NFL Super Bowl MVP Joe Namath).

Photo: Greg Howard

I really didn't care much to be a spectator. My concern was how *Happy Days* character Fonzie was going to save Richie Cunningham's ass from getting herbed, or if Arnold Horshack from *Welcome Back, Kotter* could laugh any more annoyingly.

I don't know if Dad was attempting to make me like b-ball so that I wouldn't wince at him for stomping on my favorite shows, but in '74 he put our family's cherished Spalding rubber basketball in my hand for the very first time. The rock had what we called "titties" trying to pop through the surface. Attempting to dribble an uneven sphere with mad bubbles was NOT easy.

We lived on 97th Street in a building named Westgate. The backyard had this bullshit rim that seemed like it was eleven feet in the clouds stuck on flimsy plywood that barely resembled a rectangle. Backboards are usually hung two to four feet from a mounted surface for safety reasons. Our makeshift one was nailed flush against a seven-foot concrete wall. Crash-test-dummy status.

At age seven I could barely reach this high-ass goal with my Olympic shotputs, but it didn't matter. I watched kids frolic there daily from our thirteenth-floor terrace, and although I wasn't allowed to go to "The Back" by myself just yet, I was

amped to finally be in the mix. The real jewel was spending time with Dad one-on-one. On the court he was in bliss, and his jump-shot form would've made Clyde Frazier proud. Seeing his inner soul shine was the first impression of my father that I wanted to emulate.

In 1953, my father was an eighteen-year-old b-ball fiend living in Puerto Rico. He rocked outdoors every day and impressed some coaches enough to be invited to a tryout for the Cardenales de Río Piedras of the island's Baloncesto Superior Nacional (BSN) pro league. Unfortunately, right before camp started, his single mother asked that he move with her to New York to help take care of his younger siblings. Pops arrived at 84th Street off Columbus saddened by the change in plans, but excited about experiencing ball in the Mecca.

During the 1950s, an estimated 100,000 Puerto Ricans migrated to NYC, and roughly 40,000 of them called Manhattan's Upper West Side home. Irish immigrants embedded in the neighborhood for decades weren't exactly welcoming, so aside from dealing with new weather conditions, employment/housing/educational discrimination, plus language barriers for some, many Boricuas were faced with oppression from gang violence, poverty, crime, police brutality, prejudice, and racism (and mi gente are still suffering from many of these social injustice issues seventy-plus years later, both here and on the island).

One day, my father tried calling next at a pickup run in Central Park on 86th Street. He was the only Puerto Rican there. "You want next?" one of the ballplayers asked with a smirk. "You can have the court all to yourself." Needle scratch. The Irish kids stopped their five-on-five and marched off in protest along with their friends on the side.

Alone and humiliated on the end line, my father stood in shock, then cried. He grew up on an island affectionately known as "La Isla del Encanto" (the Island of Enchantment) but was now struggling on another appropriately nicknamed "The Rotten Apple."

Yet his passion for basketball didn't dissipate.

Toward the end of the fifties, Dad got introduced to the Joan of Arc JHS Night Center. Most of the Latinos there hung among themselves, competing in table games, weight lifting, and boxing. The African Americans and Irish Americans played ball on segregated courts. There was tension in the air, and inevitably, fights would break out.

The Center eventually created a five-on-five league, and with the director's blessing, my father organized the first ethnically and racially integrated squad on the Upper West Side. They were dominant, and corralled support from multiple communities. As a result, fighting decreased in the gym. They went on to win the championship that debut season.

My father used ball as a tool for social change.

While neither the success of the Knicks nor my father's activism were giving me that *hunger* to learn the game, I was nonetheless entertained by watching cats ball out. And it seemed like in this here city, the sport was unavoidable.

Photo: Elijah Henderson

My moms, Mona García, cut hair at a salon in El Barrio. Ma would often take me to work with her. The beauty parlor was a smoky room with an old-school engraved tin ceiling, big-ass beehive hairdryers (that looked like you could turn them over and wash your clothes in them), and fat-ass raisable chairs. I would sit in them and spin around in circles until I was about to vomit the quenepas from the sidewalk fruit stand. The smell of chemical relaxers, perm juice, hair spray, etc., wasn't helping, either. Oh, and no AC. In the summer, that place was packed like the uptown 6 train at rush hour, and hotter than Death Valley, California. So, I would step out for air.

Luckily, the White Park was literally next door. The handball court was always popping with music, and the b-ball comp was bananas, attracting all the best ballplayers from El Barrio's Schaeffer League. The "Latin version of the Rucker," as local coach Santos Negrón would call it, featured regulars like future Puerto Rico national team guard Angel "Monch" Cruz, BSN champion César "Spanish Doc" Fantauzzi, BSN all-star Andrés "Corky" Ortiz, future San Antonio Spurs draft pick Hector Olivencia, and Rice HS sensation José París. Harlem's all-time scoring legend Joe "The Destroyer" Hammond, Fordham U. all-American Charlie Yelverton, and future NBA champ/New York Knick Dean "The Dream" Meminger would all battle it out there from time to time, as well. The pickup was intense, and the arguments would hit high decibels. I didn't have a clue who anybody was back then, though.

The only cat who ran there who I knew personally was nicknamed "Peachy." He'd come into the beauty parlor to hang with my moms and her customers. And I don't know this for fact, but I feel like Peachy would keep an eye on me at the park. Most times I'd be there with my cousin Joselito or my older brother Billy, but they weren't adults. I didn't have a nanny or helicopter parents like that. The community raised me. As did the asphalt.

One of my mom's regular customers was a shapely brown-skinned Boricua named Judy, who became a close friend of the family and wound up watching me from time to time as well. She would always greet me with a kiss on my lips. My body would feel flush. I was shy and would blush. My world stopped for her!

My prepubescent crush aside, I could tell Judy really loved me as if I were her own child, as did her boyfriend Pauly, a Dick Butkus–looking blond-haired 6'4" ex-semipro football player with a goatee. As mean as he looked, he was a gentle giant and, like his lady, really took to me. One day, he brought me along to a basketball game he had in the postal workers league at the Hudson Guild gym on 26th Street. It was the first time I ever witnessed people competing under the whistle. I was amazed. And intimidated. The game got heated, and cats almost started throwing joints. Pauly's team lost, and he only scored four points. As frustrated as he was, he kept it chilly-willy status and was still really kind to me.

Pauly was my first sports hero. He could've thrown me his jersey after the game and made a Coke commercial, à la "Mean" Joe Greene.

In 1972, I entered first grade at Holy Name, a Catholic school just a block away from the crib. I wasn't allowed to cross the street by myself yet, so I'd have to wait for my brother Billy to walk me home after school. He was on the sixth-grade basketball team, so I started going to his practices.

One afternoon I got amped up cuz the players decided to make me their ball boy. I didn't really know what that meant, but whatever. It beat riding pine until practice was over. They started a layup line, and my dumb ass ran on the court to join. The coach immediately instructed me to stay out of bounds. He didn't want me to get hurt, but I didn't know that, so I felt like a soggy loaf of stale bread. I put my head down and leaned my body backward, not knowing that the wall was a good five feet behind me. I must've looked like a slow-motion falling domino, landing flat on my back then clunking my dome piece on the wood floor. The whole squad broke out laughing at the top of their lungs. And in that tiny-ass gym, any sound echoed. I felt surrounded by a gospel choir of hyenas. Embarrassment would be an understatement.

I never went back to Billy's practice.

I did however see Billy play a few years later at the Duncan PAL Center in Hell's Kitchen. I was in awe of his athleticism. Mi hermano had springs on his jumper, and his right leg would bend backward into a right triangle as he'd hang in the air, releasing the ball at the height of his shot. Both my brothers were becoming immersed in NYC b-ball culture during the midseventies. Ray made the Gauchos squad when their home was the West Side Y on 63rd Street and played in the mighty Holcombe Rucker Memorial Youth

League up in Harlem. Mi hermano mayor didn't have ups like Billy, but he really knew how to use his body to create space. Ray was also ambidextrous going to the cup and basically took whatever the defense gave him.

I was observant of my brothers' athleticism and skills, though it was mostly lost on me. I was much more engaged playing with my Hot Wheels or G.I. Joe toys at the crib, or going to the Back at Westgate to play:

> —on the seesaw where'd we jump off to watch the person on the other side slam down with velocity;
> —Hot Peas & Butter, Come and Get Your Supper, a sadistic game where the player who found the hidden belt could swing it on anyone trying to run back to home base;
> —Ringalario 1, 2, 3, 1, 2, 3, 1, 2, 3, a game like Tag except we had to hold the person while saying the long-ass name plus numbers to capture them;

> —Skelsies aka Skully, an old-school game we played with bottle caps or the metal from the bottom of a desk chair leg which we'd fill with melted wax for weight and color, then shoot them with our finger into boxes we'd draw with chalk;
> —Blacula, another sadistic game where the building bully Britt who was strong as sh*t was "it," and if he caught you, he'd then punch the juice pulp out your arm until it was like a boneless chicken thigh.

Cats in my building also played two-hand-touch Nerf football, stickball with a taped-up mop handle, and street hockey where half of us didn't even have roller skates. I used the metal clip-on sh*ts over my canvas PRO-Keds, which were loud and did . . . not . . . roll. I would've been quicker running on my hand-me-down tube socks with the gigantic holes in the toe and heel. If the puck went over our fence into the backyard of the tenement buildings on 96th Street, then we had to climb over and jump a few feet down to retrieve it. There was a barking guard dog that'd race out the door, so we literally had seconds to avoid getting chased and bit.

That was safe compared to the threat of someone upstairs throwing an egg, an ice cube, or an M-80 explosive firework out their window at us. The worst was people hocking loogies then spitting from above with intent to land on our domes, or the time a neighbor peed in a saucepan on a ridiculously hot summer day and asked twenty of us, "Do you want some water?" We all yelled, "Yeah!" And we got splashed—in our faces, just like when the hardest hard rock in our building used to demand that we kneel, close our eyes, and open our mouths. Then he'd fott, wild loud, right in our grill piece. Dag.

There were bizarre moments in the Back, too. One time our ball rolled by the community room entrance. My neighbor Morris yelled out, "That's a used condom on the ground!" I didn't have the foggiest of what that was, and was curious, so . . . I picked it up. "Eww, YOU GOT THE COOTIES NOW!!!" Morris yelled at me. I replied, "Nah-ah! I got my everlasting cooties shot already!" If only my mother knew how much wild sh*t I was experiencing just thirteen floors below our apartment . . .

My low point at the Back was the day I was running around and noticed a circular area in the concrete that looked stained in deep burgundy. There was an eerie energy about it that was palpable, even if I couldn't put my finger on it. My homeboy noticed me transfixed in the moment and walked over to explain that a woman had committed suicide by jumping from her eleventh-floor window.

I had contemplated suicide after watching my father be assaulted and doing absolutely nothing instead of attempting to break up the ruckus or protect him somehow. I was too young, too scared. I froze. I would've gotten pummeled, but the thought that I should have at least tried something lingered in my mind for a while afterward. The whole experience saddened me.

Our neighbor had died immediately upon impact. I looked up and could imagine what her descent to the ground must've been like. Our building's super and maintenance man had tried to remove the blood but couldn't. That essentially ended my chapter of hanging in the backyard. I couldn't unsee that.

In 1975, my brother Ray shared a Dean "The Dream" Meminger quote with me from a 1973 *New York* magazine interview: "If you don't play ball, you can't hang out."

I didn't quite understand the nuance of that statement just yet, and Ray didn't explain much to me at that point, either, but with the zaniness going on in the Back, I gathered I ain't have much to lose trying out for the basketball team at Holy Name. I made the sixth-grade team as a fourth-grader. Don't be impressed: I don't think anyone got cut. I can't recall getting any playing time whatsoever that season. I'd be completely lost in practice, too. "Wait, which way do I run on the three-man weave again?"

We didn't even have uniforms. We used our gym class T-shirts with the school logo and went to the Army & Navy store on Broadway to get iron-on numbers on the back. Midseason the felt digits would start peeling off, and the top half would crumple up and hang on for dear life. The ref would be like, "Foul! On number . . . um . . . not sure . . ."

In 1977, I turned eleven and was still a complete burger, but I became a starter on the sixth-grade squad regardless. Against Saint Stephen of Hungary School, I had my best game—six points—plus we won 18–14. Since my teammate Kevin Buist and I were the high scorers, Mrs. Simplicio mentioned our names on the PA to the whole school during the morning announcement. That was way better than receiving a star from our teacher Mr. Mezzardi for perfect attendance (made with aluminum foil from the school kitchen).

My teammate Reginald Brignole made a huge impression on me that season. He was the most confident cat on our squad, and not just cuz he was our best player, either. Reggie always had the slick duds, like a thin tie for away games, or a new wristband for home ones, so I started wearing an Ace bandage around my knee for no reason other than to try to look cool, too. We'd hang outside together sometimes during lunch break on 97th Street, which would be closed to traffic so we could play on the street. We weren't permitted to go any farther than the corner bodega, though, where I'd buy them red one-cent fish that'd stick to my teeth for hours.

One day, Reggie invited me to sneak out, and we hit the Goat on 99th and Amsterdam. It was my first time ever playing ball on an official NYC outdoor court. We shot around on the side rims cuz the adults were running a full on the main one. I was exhilarated.

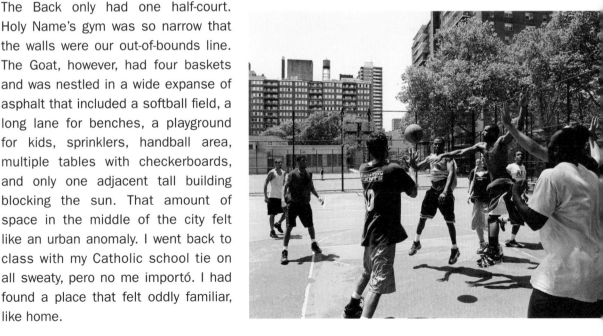

The Back only had one half-court. Holy Name's gym was so narrow that the walls were our out-of-bounds line. The Goat, however, had four baskets and was nestled in a wide expanse of asphalt that included a softball field, a long lane for benches, a playground for kids, sprinklers, handball area, multiple tables with checkerboards, and only one adjacent tall building blocking the sun. That amount of space in the middle of the city felt like an urban anomaly. I went back to class with my Catholic school tie on all sweaty, pero no me importó. I had found a place that felt oddly familiar, like home.

A few weeks later, I was back at the Goat, but not to play ball. Four of my classmates threatened to jump me if I didn't take a puff of the herb they were passing around. By this point in my life, I had already been mentally, physically, and sexually abused, so I was no stranger to getting yoked up or mapped in my face. I begrudgingly took a hit and started coughing as the smoke burned my throat. No knock on my boys, but it just wasn't my thing. At least I avoided the smackdown.

Before the end of that '77–'78 season, we had an away game downtown in the Lower East Side (LES). Reggie stole the ball, so I took off downcourt to fill the lane. Reg hit me with the no-look so lovely, and I had an uncontested breakaway layup . . . which . . . I blew. I ran back on defense and at half-court, I smacked myself. As in, I took my own hand and went palm to face mad-hard kapow status. In front of everyone. It was an impulse reaction. I had gotten so used to getting hit by bullies in my life when I did something wrong that I even inflicted the same harm on myself.

My masochistic moment aside, b-ball was *seemingly* a safe place for me, mostly because none of the bullies on my block played on the team. The most danger I'd sense would be when we'd go up by Dyckman to play against the Good Shepherd School. The Irish kids there were tough and talked mad sh*t. Maybe they were trying to intimidate us, maybe they really wanted to scrap, but nothing ever happened (and we always lost to them anyway, so their tactic worked).

While b-ball was taking the lead as a potential favorite sport, it took a backseat to baseball that summer of '78 when I was asked to be the captain of the Angelo's Braves team in Central Park's Little League. We really should've been called the Bad News Bears, just like that 1976 movie. We stayed getting shellacked, most times on shutouts. One pitcher threw a perfect game against us where none of us even reached first base. I had a decent glove, though, and got invited to the all-star game.

The week before the ASG, I was diagnosed with osteochondritis dissecans. Basically, a piece of my thigh bone had become unattached due to lack of circulation (the price I paid for wearing an Ace bandage tightly for no reason), and the only thing holding it back from entering my bloodstream was my cartilage, or so the doctors explained. I was admitted to St. Luke's Hospital, same place I was born, and stayed there for eleven days until I recovered from the operation.

Days after being released, I told my mom that I had a sharp pain on the right side of my stomach by my waist. She said, "You need to get your appendix removed." When I arrived back at St. Luke's, I told the doctor the same, and he was like, "How did you know that?" I replied, "Oh, my mother is like the best nurse in the galaxy." I was hospitalized once again, this round for seven days.

Eighteen days total on a hospital bed and two operations within three weeks at the tender age of eleven. There went my baseball season.

The following summer of '79, I hit my first, and only, career home run, but still struggled with the bat. My defense improved, though. Inspired by World Series champ Graig Nettles of the New York Yankees, I held down third base, diving left, right, and forward any chance I could get to protect the hot corner. One day at practice, this older white man introduced himself and said, "Nice glove, kid. Here . . ." and he gave me a business card with the San Francisco Giants logo on it. I wasn't sure if he was a legit scout or some creeper, though, so I never followed up.

In 1980, I moved up to Junior Pony. The coach's son played third base, so I was riding pine during preseason. Watching the Mets play at Shea Stadium while eating hot dogs was fun. Watching our squad play when I knew I was better than the kid in front of me was boring. I dipped out. My last hurrah would be tryouts that fall when I was a freshman at Brooklyn Tech HS. I struck out repeatedly and got cut. I haven't been back to play at a field since.

Baseball wasn't the only other sport that caught my interest, though. From '77–'79, I was a proud member of the Westgate Panthers football team. We never had enough players for games of eleven-on-eleven, and some kids couldn't afford full equipment, so sometimes we'd just play two-hand touch. Was good times, though. Our building went undefeated against all others in our area, including 765 Amsterdam which featured future Rock Steady Crew members DOZE of the TC5 graffiti crew and Ken Swift, who I would consider the greatest b-boy of all time.

00 19

Similar to my short-lived baseball career, when I arrived at Brooklyn Tech HS, I tried out for the football squad. I was literally the last player selected to make the team. Gone were the fun days of trying to catch color streaks on my helmet from tackling an opponent head-to-head. I was skinny, not that strong, not particularly fast, and not crazy athletic. The returning free safety was twenty-five pounds heavier than me and ran the forty-yard dash in two eye blinks. I was looking at riding the bench, but unlike baseball, I'd be outside in the cold. F that. I quit. As in, I went to one practice, then I broke out.

I loved playing sports, though. Retired from baseball and football by age fourteen, and street hockey never having had a chance, I turned to the love that was always standing right in front of my face . . .

# THE BODY Rock

"Bobby, your shot is flat with no rotation, and you look like a frog when you jump. Coquí, coquí!"

Dad had a friend who lived off the corner of Seaman and Cumming Street. Dead ass, those were the names. We'd all shoot around at nearby Inwood Park. When my father critiqued my game, I was all ears. There was no footage to study what I looked like. I had never been to a camp to learn the fundamentals, and none of the coaches at Holy Name pulled me to the side to teach individual skills. There was no such thing as personal trainers back then. Any jewel Pops dropped about how to improve, I listened.

In the fall of 1980, I turned fourteen and became a freshman at Brooklyn Tech High School. I was three points shy of qualifying for Bronx Science, and the principal at Holy Name thought so highly of my academics that he offered to get me into the city's top-rated public school, Stuyvesant.

Both options would've required summer classes, so I settled for Tech, which was kind of a zoo with six thousand students crammed into an eight-story building that took up an entire block. The caged staircases were hectic. I used them to work on my calf muscles as I climbed to the upper floors for boring classes like foundry.

I looked forward to gym class every day. The teacher had jokes, saying he had extra peanut shells and rubber bands if anyone needed a jock-strap cup. He'd roll out ancient leather basketballs that barely had any grooves we could line our fingers up on, and let us rock. My classmate James Alston from Crown Heights, BK, had a smooth game. He was always dipped up with a pressed cherry-red tee with matching high-top Chucks, laced b-boy style over the eyelets, not under. That was an unwritten way of knowing who listened to hip hop (not that we called it that yet) and who didn't. James and I would often be on the same squad. I wasn't much of a scorer, but I knew how to set the table and feed him.

Photo: Carlos Arias

James invited me to these Saturday-morning workouts at Crispus Attucks Playground on Fulton and Classon in "Bed-Stuy Do or Die," as everyone called it back then. KRS's line, *"Manhattan keeps on making it, Brooklyn keeps on taking it"* was no joke. I had already gotten vicked for my umbrella in Fort Greene by eight dudes from Farragut who circled me, which was light. I saw cats heading home from Tech in their socks. I wanted to meet James, but I had to be strategic in Bruknahm. I put on my brother Bill's Nike fat-belly swoosh Blazers, which were a little too big on me plus beat up, but that was the trick. Wear something that would make me look like a ballplayer, but not be too fresh out the box to attract getting burped for my kicks. James's coach welcomed me, and we all did layup drills together. Going to the cup and slapping boards on a defender was a big deal, especially if you couldn't dunk. A two-hand clap was even iller.

A few weeks into the semester, I walked into science class and two dudes ran out their seats and put me in a yoke. One said, "Is he a homeboy?" to his mans, then, "Are you a homeboy?" to me. They were from Crown Heights, too, so James knew them. My gym class crony looked at both and said, "Chill, b. Bobby's cool, man. He plays ball . . ." and just like that, they took their arms off my neck, asked me, "Yo, you alright?" and never bothered me again. I sh*t you not.

If only I could have told all the bullies in my preteen years that I played ball and to just leave me the f*ck alone. That would've made my childhood a lot easier.

Because of the heavy student body, Tech had ten periods. Cats either went first to eighth, or third to tenth. I was in that latter group, which meant that we got out of school at four p.m. Wack sauce, especially when fall turned into winter and the sun started dipping out earlier. Playing ball kept getting more and more important to me, and since there was no freshman squad to try out for, I started cutting class so I could be out and about searching for a run.

My partner in crime that winter was my former Holy Name teammate Alix Achille, who was one year younger than me but stronger, more athletic, and a little ahead in skills. Alix was Haitian, and could speak English, Creole, plus a little Spanish, too, all three with a bit of a stammer in his tongue. He loved b-ball so much that it quietly fueled my hunger as well. We started rolling thick, like syrup on the top pancake. We shoveled snow. When it was raining, we just put our ponchos on. We were getting our shots up. Daily. Without fail.

Alix and I both idolized *New York Post* First Team all-city HS senior Mario Elie, who also lived in Westgate. My brother Ray told me when "The Jedi" won the MVP at the Goat Tournament, the trophy was so big, it didn't even fit in our building's entrance. My boy Greg Brown shared that when he and Mario's older brother Clark, who was also nasty, took Mario to the pickup run at Central Park for the first time, they left the other squad on their donut, 40–zip. Note that the comp there was legit in that era. They told Greg, "Don't ever bring lil' bro back here again. He's not welcome!" The Elie siblings were also legendary down at West 4th Street, winning the tournament there five years consecutively as members of Harlem USA.

Mario was three years ahead of me at Holy Name, and I remember the first time I saw him play for our school. His team lost, and he had played so hard, he started crying from the emotion. Jump forward to his senior year at nationally ranked Power Memorial, though, and it was the other teams who were shedding tears . . . from getting dunked on. Repeatedly. Bong BONG!

Alix and I went to a game one afternoon. The whole squad rocked Converse Dr. Js in white/purple, which no store carried, so it was like being in an elevator with Michael Jackson (as in none of your friends would believe it happened). During the layup line, they played the Treacherous Three's "Body Rock," which no radio station was playing. Rap records being heard anywhere except the hood was unthinkable in that era. The whole experience was surreal. Mario had crazy hops, yummed it two hands every chance he could get, played D, and fought tooth and nail to get the W. Wasn't a surprise to any of us on the block when he went on to win three NBA rings in the nineties with the Houston Rockets and San Antonio Spurs.

Although Mario was a familiar face from the building, I was petro to be on his squad the few times I played pickup with him. "You a *non*, Bobby!" he'd yell at me. NYC b-ball culture was broken into two distinct populations: ballplayers and *non*ballplayers. "Pass me the rock!" I'd hit the panic button and turn the ball over, which would frustrate him even more.

Mario took a liking to Alix, though. They had the Haitian connection, plus homeboy had potential. Mario explained to him that you could always tell if you had shot the ball correctly with the right rotation if it bounced directly back to you. Alix shared Mario's golden words with me as if they were Isaac Newton's First Law of Motion.

**THE BODY ROCK**

Our testing ground was the Goat. There were never any nets, so trying to hear that swish sound *whap* was impossible, but great for our experiment. Our goal was the back  rim—didn't matter from the corner, the top of the key, whatever. We kept track of whether the ball came back to us slightly to the right or left, as if we were scientists trying to prove a theory. Then we would adjust our release accordingly. When we both got consistent, it was time to leave the block and branch out to other courts. You ain't sh*t if you can only get nice at your own park. That was unwritten NYC law.

Riverside Church had the mightiest youth team in the world at the time. Chris Mullin, "Pearl" Washington, Walter Berry, Kenny Smith, Mark Jackson, and too many other HS all-Americans out of New York who would wind up in the NBA had all worn the Hawks's coveted flap jacket and bag at one point or another. Reggie Carter put that program on the map before leading St. John's to the 1979 NCAA Tournament Elite Eight. The backup guard for the Knicks in '80–'81 was raised right up the block from us in the Douglass projects, so me and Alix would see him around the way. Naturally, we were inspired to follow in his footsteps, so we tried out for Riverside's squad for ages thirteen to fifteen.

Alix did his thing, scored a few times, and followed the drills smoothly. I didn't at all and got cut. As we were putting on our coats to break out, the founder and director of the Riverside Church Hawks, Ernie Lorch, a tall white man who was supposedly a millionaire lawyer, asked Alix to join him in the locker room for a moment. I had unfortunately experienced sexual predators in my preteens, so my Spidey senses went off. I stayed some distance behind and watched from the hallway to make sure my boy wasn't gonna be violated. Mr. Lorch asked Alix to undress and turn his body a full 360 degrees, stared at his physique for a few secs, then told him to get dressed and he could go. When Alix came out, I asked him what happened. "Lorch said he wanted to see how athletic my body was," Alix stuttered out. "I made the team, but f*ck that. I'm not going back . . ."

We walked the mile from 121st and Claremont back to the Goat in silence.

Alix and I were both sincerely nice, polite kids, but trying to find an indoor court we were welcome in during that winter was a chore, so we started sneaking into Columbia University's Levien Gym. The first hustle was hoping a student was checking IDs at the entrance, cuz they'd usually be stressed the f out with their head deep in a book, paying us no mind as we slid through the turnstile. When a security guard was up front, we'd check downstairs to see if any doors were left unlocked from an event the night before. If that didn't fly, we would walk all the way to a garage entrance on Amsterdam and 119th where no one ever asked us where we were headed. Down the ramp, past the parked cars, down another level, over oil puddles and boiler pipes . . . I'm not sure how we ever figured out that one of the doors would lead us to the locker room, but as if we had the architect's blueprint memorized, we eventually found our way to the gym. And that was always worth getting our dogged-up kicks dirtier for.

The Levien's three full courts with fiberglass backboards, thick NCAA nets, and freshly waxed wood floors were somewhat of a palace compared to what we were used to. The Y on 63rd had an elevated track over the playing area, which negated corner shots. Stone Gym on 120th had wall-mounted steam radiators that protruded over the out-of-bound lines. Central Baptist on 92nd had slippery floor tiles, some of which were missing, with low ceilings that would block any eighteen-footer with the quickness. Oh, and no heat. I saw fog breath out my mouth one time, and not because I had put garlic powder on my slice of pizza. It was *that* cold down there.

These indoor spots had open gym hours for youth, and they'd be packed. In contrast, at the Levien we could play pickup against super-doo-doo comp or go on the side rims to work on our game. I wasn't making much progress, though. I didn't have any instruction, and you can't really get better playing against scrubs. Meanwhile, I was failing seven classes at Brooklyn Tech, all because I was constantly cutting out to play ball. I had been a straight-A student at Holy Name, so my parents were oblivious to my freshman-year exploits because they trusted me to do the right thing. I was on a path to being ineligible to try out as a sophomore the following fall semester, so something had to change.

Enter Earl Manigault.

Photo: © Charlie Samuels, 1990

★ BOBBITO'S BOOK OF B-BALL BONG BONG

# THE MAIN INGREDIENT

Earl Manigault aka "The Goat" (born September 7, 1944) was one of the greatest ballplayers Harlem ever produced. As a preteen, the high-jumping guard broke NYC's junior high school scoring record with fifty-seven in one game. As a teenager, Manigault was a star for Benjamin Franklin HS and led them to the PSAL finals. He transferred to nationally recognized Laurinburg Institute (in North Carolina) where seventy-five colleges recruited him, including perennial NCAA champions UCLA. He wound up at Johnson C. Smith University for a season, was unhappy there, and returned north.

Although Manigault never shined as he could've on the scholastic circuit because of academic challenges, it was in the parks where he really made a name for himself. There was the Holcombe Rucker Youth League game where Earl yoked it on three 6'8" bigs waiting for him in the paint. Note: the Goat was only 6'1". Little dudes weren't dunking like that in the fifties. The crowd threw chairs onto the court for five minutes in hysteria. The contest didn't resume for a half hour!

Someone once bet Earl sixty bucks that he couldn't hit a reverse dunk thirty times in a row, so he threw down thirty-six consecutively and took the dough . . . easily. Six-time NBA champion Kareem Abdul-Jabbar used to play pickup with Earl Manigault in their youth, and once called him "the best basketball player his size in the history of New York City."

Unfortunately, just as the hood made Earl a legend, it also sucked him up. Manigault never made it to the NBA. Instead, he wound up hooked on heroin and turned to crime to support his habit. He spent a few years in prison, and when released, his reputation was enough to earn a 1971 tryout with the ABA's Utah Stars, though he was cut as his best years on the court were long gone.

In the seventies, Manigault started the Goat Tournament in Harlem and eventually moved the action to 99th and Amsterdam, right across the street from where I lived. Future NBA players Albert King and Jeff Ruland suited up as youngins, as did players Earl knew from the Rucker. There was also the local royalty of the Elie brothers and Reggie Carter, whose little brother Darryl would wind up playing D1 at UMass and was a regular, too. The court caught citywide rep, and everyone started calling it "The Goat" aka "Goat Park."

Once the weather warmed up in the spring of 1981, I too became a regular at the Goat. Earl was there often as he lived nearby. I had heard all these stories about his legend, so having him watch me play was inspiring. Some days he'd show me trick passes off the back of his knee, or we'd just shoot around. His form was interesting. He'd place the ball over his left eye before releasing, even though he was right-handed. Sh*t went in with perfect rotation, so didn't matter.

I had the pleasure to run a couple of fulls with Earl, even though I rarely saw him play competitively due to heart conditions and prior surgeries he'd had. That all said, it was still ridiculous to see him dunk, considering what his body had gone through as a recovered heroin addict and someone who had been incarcerated just ten years prior. He told me he had never shot junk in his legs, though, only his arms.

That tidbit might have been the most revealing fact Earl ever shared with me. He otherwise didn't say much, least not to me. Some of his teeth had fallen out due to his drug use, and I didn't know if that made him self-conscious or not.

The Goat was a mythical mentor at the park who led by example, with an approachable and kind demeanor. There was a melancholy aura to him, though. As a tournament director, he was providing a positive platform for recreation to hundreds of youths every summer with his "walk away from drugs" messaging. As a ballplayer in the fifties and sixties, though, the hard truth was that he had been an underachiever, someone who never reached his full potential.

While Earl never had to convince me not to drink or smoke—I was already on that—the lesson he did indirectly impress upon me was that in life, we can make some great decisions, and some wrong and hurtful ones. What side did I want to stand on?

There were older cats who would see me in the park in the morning, then again in the

afternoon, then again when the sun was going down, and they'd say, "I see you, Bobby. You putting in work. If I had the chance to do it all again, man . . ." And it was then, at age fourteen, that I decided I never wanted to live with regret. I didn't wanna look back at my life and think that I should've tried harder, or that I hadn't given it my all. I stopped cutting class at Brooklyn Tech altogether. And I decided during that spring of 1981 to dedicate my mind, body, and soul to being the best basketball player I could ever be.

So, thank you, Earl Manigault. Thank you.

Basketball became my religion. Goat Park became my place of worship.

The cult of devoted ballplayers I met and played with there was a motley crew, a disparate collection of characters. Steve Cohen was a professor of Russian studies at Princeton who was tight with Earl and would support his tournament however he could. Steve wore an Ace elastic brace around his chest and shoulder that limited the mobility of his shooting arm, yet he'd still compete. His health was not going to stop him from playing.

There was also Bob, who I thought might've been unhoused. I wasn't sure. Either way, he was a little unhinged. His BO could blow out a candle, so cats would only put him down when there wasn't enough bodies for a full. One morning, I saw Bob jerking off in broad daylight on the bench in the alley. I don't remember seeing him much after that. Or maybe I just blocked his presence out my head.

Cano was a jolly old man who would only show up in his dress shoes and church socks when the courts were emptying at night. With a can of beer in his left hand, the loan shark would hit consecutive one-hand set shots, sometimes up to twenty in a row, taking sips of Schaeffer in between each one. The tipsier he got, the more accurate he became. Chico was another happy-go-lucky cat in his forties who was in the army reserve and had the grip of a kingsnake. He'd hold the ball with two hands then taunt, "See if you can rip it from me, Bobby!" Mission impossible—not once was I successful.

Photo: Henry Chalfant

Cano and Chico were two of many Puerto Rican ballplayers at the Goat. Nelson aka "Sucio" had an accurate lean-back set shot, but only on the low rim, and was always clad in cutoff dungarees over his gray sweatpants, no matter how hot it was. Freddy Roman was an all-city baseball player for Brooklyn Tech whose jumper resembled a knuckleball pitch. He used the soft backboard well, though. My favorite fellow Latino there was Woody, a member of the Rock Steady Crew. Crazy Legs, Ken Swift, and Frosty Freeze would be breakin' on linoleum by the swings, and Woody would drift off with his white gloves on so he could play half-court with me. A true b-boy, he never tied his sneakers because he had the fat laces looking fly. One day his shoe flew off as he was going to the hole. He still made the layup in his socks, though. We all busted out laughing.

Music industry cats were regulars, too. Reggie Wells was a popular radio disc jockey who let it be known by always rockin' his WBLS varsity jacket, which nobody else had. Was so fresh, he wouldn't even put it down to shoot with his Bob McAdoo form. Would've gotten dirty! Rob Hill, who was also my neighbor at Westgate, was slow on his defensive slides, but quick in the mind. He signed the god Rakim to his first recording contract on his Zakia label, which was named after his daughter. In 1987, Island/4th & B'way released the Eric B. & Rakim debut album *Paid in Full*, which eventually went platinum.

Tracey Townes and Sean Nelson repped for the ladies at the Goat. They both held their own against the dudes since they never had enough for a women-only run. Tracey was a portrait of strong fundamentals, while Sean, who had like five brothers who could ball, was a slasher with a little bit of a handle. I dug watching them rock out.

There was a bevy of oversized players. John "Bagley" had crazy hang time, even though his vert was only like two inches. He'd never finish on the side of the backboard he was on, opting to protect the ball by laying it up with a reverse. Was like watching Silver Surfer glide on air. Wave Ivey didn't have ups either, yet everyone always wanted to pick him when choosing squads. "Wavey" knew how to feed people like a soup kitchen on Gobble-Gobble Day, and rarely turned the ball over.

I loved how certain cats were given nicknames, like left-handed "Buggs" who probably caught that at first cuz heads were snapping on his buck teeth, but his game was so nice, the name transformed into something cool. He always got picked up for next the moment he walked in the park. I never knew his real name, same as "Lefty" who had an unstoppable sidestep to the rack, "E" whose midrange was ridiculous high-percentage, and "Cheese" who was a rebound machine in his pleated postal-worker shorts during lunch break.

There were three Jeffs at the Goat. The toughest defender was just Jeff. The highest-jumping became "Light-Skin Jeff." The smoothest player of the three I personally called "Slinky Jeff." Might've been the first person I ever nicknamed. I LOVED his game. The right-hander shot the ball from the left side of his face à la Earl Manigault, and his handle was like them wooden spinning-top toys with the string. I never knew when Slinky was gonna shoot. I'd guard him and literally be in awe.

Everyone I've mentioned so far was older than me. There was a whole group of kids my age at the Goat, too, though. Steve was a one-hand bandit, which was frowned upon, but even though everyone in the park knew he was always going right, no one could stop him. And he'd finish with a flush. Hong! Steve wound up playing D1 at the University of Hawaii years later. Maurice had the silky jumper, and would land gingerly to not scuff his Blazers. He always had on kicks fresh out the box. I didn't know how he or anyone afforded to buy so many pairs. Barry "Bistro" Clark was another sharp dresser, head to toe, whose

Courtesy of Gary Clark

game matched his flashiness. Barry's little brother Gary was something of a child prodigy who could dribble under one leg three times wild low and so quickly it looked like a Chinese ping-pong match. I honestly thought he was going to wind up in the NBA down the road. He showed that much potential at a young age.

All these dudes were better than me, but none of them were as good as Richie Simmonds, the best player in our age group at the Goat. The 6'2" lanky guard would go on to be the number one scorer in the '83–'84 Catholic League his senior season at All Hallows HS. Richie was a lefty sharpshooter who defied everything my father had told me about the benefit of rotation. His shot had none. Flat and no arc, like a dead fish tossed in the air. But sh*t would go in. And in. And IN!

Cano could hit twenty in a row easy, but that was with no D. E could do the same in a game, though not so much against the topflight comp at the park. Richie on the other hand was deadeye unstoppable against whoever, and I honestly felt like his field goal percentage at the Goat was 99 percent. He introduced me to Booty's Up, where we'd play 21 with up to ten or more players, no teammates, every man for himself. Whoever had low at the end of the game would have to bend over at the fence while the rest took turns throwing the ball at their boonkey. I unfortunately caught the Spalding logo stinging my butt cheeks more than a few times. Richie, however, won every game, day in and day out.

I do not condone violence, force, intimidation, or verbal abuse to improve one's game whatsoever, so I hate admitting that playing Booty's Up with Richie *did* make me a better ballplayer. I played harder to avoid getting hit with the ball at the end. And naturally, since I was competing against more skilled comp at the Goat than the Levien gym's doo-doo pickup run, I slowly started understanding how to score a little better. One day, I was beating this hothead in a game of 21, and then I pulled off a fancy move for another bucket on him. Homeboy took the ball and threw that sh*t right at my face from ten feet away. I had been bullied so much in my preteens that I had no fight left in me. I was also a former altar boy on some Catholic "turn the other cheek" programming. I did absolutely nothing in response but hope that it wouldn't escalate. Luckily, we just finished the game, and I won, but very timidly.

Yeah, the Goat was my church, though that didn't mean that park was always a safe space. There was a hard rock, never knew his name, who'd always run with his T-shirt off, even when it wasn't quite summer weather yet. He was cut up like Bruce Lee with the build of NFL star Earl Campbell, and he wanted all of us to know it. One time someone dared argue with him about who had next, and this diesel cat dumped the garbage can right in the middle of the court. "If I don't play, none of y'all muh'f*ckers gonna play . . ." Mic drop. Nobody said sh*t to him after that.

Even though the 24th police precinct was two hundred feet away, there were drugs and weed openly being bought and sold from the bench right outside the fenced-in court. That always seemed to move quietly, and posed no immediate threat to us playing. In sharp contrast, dudes getting drunk were the worst, cuz they'd smash their empty bottles on the court. Why, yo? What was the point? Since I was usually first to arrive, I'd pick up the glass pieces one by one. I was used to upkeep, having shoveled snow from the prior winter, so it was no biggie. No dis on the Parks & Rec staff, but they weren't going to clean the mess anytime in the foreseeable future. There were already wide cracks in the asphalt that were twist-your-ankle traps for years, and two of the

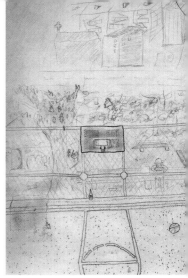

From my 1981 freehand drawing class

four main screws on the northwest rim had been loose for months from heads dunking and hanging on it. The height was lower than regulation to begin with, so the angle of the front made it nine and a half feet. With a forgiving bounce, an off shot still had a great chance of going in. Maybe that was Cano's secret; he'd always pick that court to shoot around.

Courtesy of U. of Texas, Rio Grande Valley

Danger, neglect, and the ball being thrown at me like dodgeball aside, the Goat became my sanctuary, my home away from home. My friends would call the crib and if my mother answered the phone, she'd say, "Bobby's at the Goat." Even if I had gone to the Olympia Theater on 107th Street to catch a flick, I'd eventually wind up back there anyhow. No other form of entertainment in my mind could compete, especially when the upper-echelon players would pop up, like Bruce King who averaged thirty-one points in '73–'74 for Pan American University (now U. of Texas, Rio Grande Valley). The forty-sixth pick in the NBA draft by the New Orleans Jazz didn't come often, but when he did? Man, he'd put the fog lights on. Cats would get lit up!

Gerald Erasme was the starting PG and team captain as a senior at Power Memorial HS in '79–'80, with juniors Mario Elie and future Basketball Hall of Fame inductee Chris Mullin on the wings. Imagine the options. Mullin transferred to Xaverian after the season started, but Gerald finished strong, being voted the school's Athlete of the Year. The 5'10" guard then played at Syracuse as a walk-on,

Mario Elie #34, Chris Mullin #44, Gerald Erasme #20, Jesse Fong #40

and one day he came to the Goat geared up with the Orangemen's warm-up pants. I had never seen anything D1-official up close and personal. That experience gave me hope, like someone from our park who was the same height as me and wasn't dunking could still exceed expectations. Gerald had the super-high dribble which would bait defenders to reach, then he'd shake them down for their lunch money with the "Whop-whop, bye-bye! I'm going to the Baja, cya!" I wanted to be *just like him*.

Another former Power Memorial guard came through one day to run. His name was Jesse Fong. He was the first Chinese player I ever saw, and he rocked like he was raised in Harlem. On one play, he penetrated the lane, jumped, spread his legs super wide to draw attention, then did a two-hand pass between his knees to a teammate five feet behind him at the foul line. I was like, *What the f*ck was THAT?*

Courtesy of Ray Diaz

A few weeks later, Ray Diaz picked me up for his squad before a five-on-five at the Goat. Ray was a senior at Norman Thomas HS and was recruited to play at 1978 D2 champion Cheyney State by future Hall of Fame coach John Chaney. The seventeen-year-old was already playing pro in Puerto Rico, too. On a three-on-two fast break, the lefty guard hit our teammate cutting right. The player hit Ray right back with a bad pass that was too high. I was trailing, and I don't know how Ray saw me, but the wizard tapped the ball backward so that sh*t landed right in my pocket for a fifteen-footer. It was like watching the Harlem Globetrotters circle, except I was participating in the magic instead of passively spectating. That was the first time I had experienced what people called "court sense." I honestly thought Ray had eyes in the back of his neck, or a rearview mirror on his eyebrow.

Later that day, it was time for scrubs like me to chill on the side, because one by one, all the best players from our hood were walking through the gate. Edwin "Coco" Greene showed up first. He lived in Westgate, and used to run the fourteen flights of stairs in our building, ride a fix bike, plus walk to D'Agostino Supermarket to buy Coco Rico soda (his favorite) with ankle weights on, all to build power in his legs. If there was a testament to strength training, he was it. Coco had explosive hops, and when he wasn't trying to flush it on someone's forehead, the lefty could score at will. He dropped seventy-three points in a tournament out in Kentucky, yet never finished high school. His game was college material, but he lived outside that frame.

Then Ronnie Ryer showed up; he had played at Wichita State and had the Shockers's MTXE (Mental Toughness, Extra Effort) game shorts on, meaning . . . playtime was over. Trailing behind him was his little-not-so-little brother Tommy, who supposedly scored one hundred points in a game while behind bars doing time at Rikers. Must've been family day, cuz next up was 6'9" Cliff Morgan, who would go on to play D1 at U. of Tennessee at Chattanooga, and his older sibling Bruce, who was a tough 6'3" defender. Someone must've put the bat signal up in the sky, cuz the last two heads to show up were . . . drumroll, please . . . Clark and Mario Elie.

Clark Elie was royalty at the Goat, and by no means played in the shadow of his NBA-bound little brother. If anything, it was the other way around. Clark had played D3 at City College and led them to the CUNY finals in 1976. Every year the "point god" got better and better, so by the time he was in his midtwenties, he was a pro-level ballplayer who thrived on the asphalt.

Five-time West 4th champion Clark Elie

Ray Diaz and Clark Elie chose squads. I called last next, knowing I wouldn't be picked, and copped a comfy squat on the fence that would let me lean back since it wasn't attached to the pole. I took out the mental notebook . . .

00:33

"Shoot for first . . . Our ball . . . Check . . ."

On Clark's first possession, he dribbled into the lane, pumped the ball like he was going to pass to the wing, then swung it back to his chest, raised his hand to rim level, and finger-rolled the pill so high, it hit the backboard over the box before going in for a bucket. "Two–zip . . ." Anytime Clark scored, he'd run back on D shaking his head up and down, almost as a statement to the defender, *You can't guard me, b. Trust me.* He was half man/half bobblehead.

More people started showing up to watch. The energy in the air felt like a tournament game uptown, except this was just a pickup run. An unforgettable one for me personally, especially when Mario Elie went baseline on one play. He loved going to his left, taking that extra power dribble so he could jump off his left leg and take flight with his right knee in the air for the boof. That's what everyone in the park was anticipating. We had seen it too many times. Somehow, Bruce Morgan jumped as high as Mario, and caught him on the boards. Pang! Getting rubbed indoors on fiberglass is a much different sound than getting pinned to a metal rectangle outdoors, with a crowd of shocked hooligans screaming, "Oooh!"

Clapping boards on layups. Deceptive ballhandling. Trick passes. Blocking your man's shot on the backboard. Scoring at will. Going hard. Having individual style without disrespecting the fundamentals. Gaining hood rep. Earning a nickname. Playing in front of an audience with exceptional b-ball IQ. There were all these idiosyncratic nuances to the game in NYC that I was soaking in. I wanted more. I had to get better. At the Goat, I had all the inspiration I could imagine and want directly across the street from where I lived. I didn't know what the missing pieces were, but I was open to the universe to guide me there . . .

# SOUL
# FOOD

Courtesy of the DOME Project

The summer of 1981 arrived. I had played pickup daily for nine months straight, so was amped to play organized for the first time since my Holy Name CYO days. I wasn't really fundamentally prepared, mentally or physically, but based on a growing belief that I shouldn't fear failure, I tried out for Riverside and once again got sliced with the quickness. I then pivoted to a couple of tryouts for local teams on the Upper West Side I had heard about.

The DOME Project had a tiny gym a few flights up at their center on 80th Street off Broadway, right around the corner from Zabar's, a store celebrated for its bagels, fish, and cheeses. I always thought that block smelled funny. DOME stood for Developing Opportunities through Meaningful Education, which I thought was fly, so I just held my breath. I don't think anyone got cut at tryouts. The staff just placed players on various teams that would be fair. Their goal was participation, particularly with at-risk and disadvantaged youth.

The DOME tournament was played on 84th Street between Columbus and Amsterdam, the block my father had moved to when he first landed in NYC from Puerto Rico twenty-eight years prior. The schoolyard had sh*tty backboards and rims, slopes throughout the unlevel court, and other signs of urban blight. Our squad's T-shirts had hand-drawn numbers on the back and an illustration of a player screen-printed on the front. Was a far cry from my brother Billy's gorgeously designed Duncan PAL mint-green tee with the official logo, but I didn't care about none of that. I was grateful to DOME for granting me my first step into the fabled world of NYC summer ball.

00 37

Of course, I didn't start. Brian Batchelor was on the opposing squad and was torching us. The next two teams were on the sidelines watching, along with a few roughnecks from up the block, so the park was packed. I was nervous. Minutes into the second quarter, the scorekeeper yelled out, "Sub!" and the ref signaled me into the game. On my very first play, I ripped this kid at half-court, and jetted toward our basket for a breakaway. When I turned around to check if my layup went in, all I saw was Brian Batchelor's five pair of socks and Converse Dr. Js at my eye level. He pinned my shot on the backboard—stupid hard. I can still hear the crowd howling.

Brian had initiated me into a secret society. I was ready for more.

I also tried out for the Douglass projects community center on 104th Street. Our family had lived in 865 Columbus right next to the gym when I was a newborn. By '81, though, that area had developed a rough rep, especially on the Manhattan Avenue side where there'd been a few drug-related murders. Even though I was a little intimidated, I knew the get-by code: mind your business, be aware of your surroundings but don't get caught staring at nobody, don't look like a sucker, and don't count any bills out your pocket on the street. I never had any ducats anyhow, so that last one was easy.

The Douglass gym was the size of a baby's bassinet. Like the top of the key lines might've touched each other. The temperature in the room was easily Bikram yoga status.

The exit door was left wide open for the hope of cross-ventilation. Regardless, I sweated like a racehorse during tryouts, and made the squad. Our coach, Kelsey Stevens, put us in the Rucker Memorial division for ages thirteen to fifteen. The late Mr. Holcombe Rucker had invented the idea of outdoor summer leagues for kids in 1946. The community activist and educator passed away in 1965, and a few years later the city named the courts at 155th and Eighth Avenue in his honor. Legend.

I wore my brother Ray's hand-me-down Holcombe Rucker Memorial T-shirt with pride, even as it was falling apart with holes under the arms and around the neck. So, imagine how I felt when I earned an eggplant-colored Rucker shirt with the PONY logo and #11 on the back on opening day at Mt. Morris Park in Harlem. Man . . . I was speeding. I felt official, like this was some exclusive sh*t. I literally held the uni to my nose to smell the fresh screen-printing job and Russell Athletic 50/50 cotton/polyester–blend material. The scorer's table put the Treacherous Three's "The Body Rock" 12" vinyl on the record player for our layup line, just like how I saw Mario Elie and his Power Memorial squad get down. I got amped! I never did drugs, but entering real-deal uptown b-ball culture mixed with hip hop for the first time was the closest feeling I had at that point to being intoxicated. I caught the bug. I was gonna be married to the playground for life.

The comp sobered my scrub-ass up quickly. I went on my donut in my debut, did the same when we played at Colonel Young on 145th, and stayed on my goose egg the entire season. Opponents would talk smack, "I'm gonna rip you, whiteboy," and I'd want to reply, *I'm not white, I'm Puerto Rican*, but I'd be too shook. During our last game at Dyckman, I hit a runner late in the game on that hot-ass, no-shade, light-blue-and-yellow-painted court, and my body swarmed with adrenaline.

I had scored in the Holcombe Rucker Memorial Youth League. That was a building block for confidence, even if it took six games across three tournament locations to get there.

I carried that back to the Upper West Side, where I was playing in the Goddard Riverside Tournament at PS 84's schoolyard. On the opposite side of the caged court, there were also two biddie rims by the handball wall that were so low we all could play above the rim. I had more fun playing 21 where only dunks were allowed than suiting up for the tourney. My forearms and wrists would hurt afterward, pero como dicen en español, "Vale la pena."

My GRT teammate was Richie Simmonds, and just like he'd win all our games of Booty's Up, "99%" made sure we took Ws all the way to the final. I'd injured my hand on the biddie rims days before, but no way was I gonna miss my first chance at a chip, so I started practicing lefty jumpers. Felt awkward, but it started to click.

On the opposing squad was Joe Cifone aka "Pasta," who was my boy and the deadliest shooter at PS 84. Rumor had it his father was in the Mafia and got locked up, so even though Pasta was the only white player out there, no one talked smacked to him. His teammate was high-jumping Darnell, a lefty who would miss more in-game dunks than he made, but loved trying anyway and we all encouraged him either way.

Richie and Pasta traded baskets in a shootout. Miraculously, I contributed ten points, all with my left, which was the first time I had ever recorded double figures in any category, except maybe turnovers. Our squad won, but honestly, that didn't matter to me. I wasn't down with the saying, *Winning isn't everything, it's the only thing.* I wanted to play well, get an "Ooh!" and an "Ah!" from the cats on the fence, and just be part of a beautiful movement that was pulling me in like a magnet. Playing ball was enriching my soul, so I was winning either way, no matter the final score.

Courtesy of the DOME Project

Playing in tournaments was like sprinkles on a cake: delicious but not the foundation of the dessert, which for me was still being at the Goat. My Westgate neighbor Lincoln Parker was taking notice of me there. Linc was short, but a former stickup kid, so he didn't take no sh*t from nobody. "Zinc Oxide" was a little older than me and took me under his wing. My brothers had mostly stopped playing ball by '81, so it was nice to have a mentor-like figure on the court.

Linc was a lockdown defender who was playing in the King Towers Tournament in the Foster projects that summer, which surpassed the Rucker Pro as the illest spot to see b-ball in Harlem. After his games, he'd wear his red top with the huge white star on the front to the Goat, and tell me stories about how the announcer Anthony Gumbs aka "The Amazing Gumby" was giving out nicknames. Future UNLV star Richie Adams became "The Animal." Gumby called future two-time NCAA Player of the Year Walter Berry "The Truth." Billy Sadler, a three hundred–plus-pound power forward with a nasty handle, transformed into "Big Daddy Boogie."

Lincoln would also tell me how Gumby would use imagination on the mic: "Apjak just leaped six stories to pin that shot to the boards!" and then comment on players who weren't dressed right: "You don't ball with black socks; this ain't Sunday school!" Linc's mind would be lit up telling me about it, and I'd be on a b-ball high.

"Snap out of it, Bobby, and guard up."

Lincoln loved destroying me in one-on-one. I had a slight height advantage, but didn't know how to use it. Meanwhile, he was quicker, stronger, had a better pull-up off the dribble, and was waaay hungrier.

"Too much French pastries, Bobby . . ."

He was absolutely right that if I had a choice between a fancy move with no finish and a basic bucket that conserved energy for defense, I was choosing the former.

". . . and you play too Catholic . . ."

Those words, verbatim, still echo in my head. I was indeed a soft-boiled egg inside. Linc sat me down one day and said if I wanted to get better, I had to get, in his words, "the eye of the tiger." I didn't know nothing about having a killer instinct, though. Until I met Ron Matthias.

Me (front) and Ron Matthias (fourth in line)

Central Baptist had a community team as well as a summer camp. I joined both. For a whole week, we did nothing but learn basketball, switching from station to station for instruction on how to box out, do defensive slides, two-hand chest passes, etc. At night we scrimmaged so that we could put these new fundamentals into action.

Just as I was fortunate to have Richie Simmonds as a teammate at Goddard Riverside, at Central Baptist Camp I found myself in the backcourt with a 6'2" wrecking machine named Ron Matthias. Both Richie and Ron were unstoppable. The difference was that . . . Ron was ruthless. He had that take-no-prisoners attitude, stick a knee in the chest of his defender for daring to attempt to draw an offensive charge vibe. I was playing for the fun and joy of the sport. Ron had a thirst to score on every possession, like, *Tricks are for kids.*

A few years later, word got back to me that Ron Matthias scored one hundred points in the Upward Fund winter league in Harlem. In a Holcombe Rucker Memorial game at Dyckman, Ron showed up at halftime and still dropped forty-two. On one play, the killer beat future Indiana Pacers draft pick Sean Couch off the dribble, only to find future NBA journeyman Bob McCann and future NBA All-Star Rik Smits, who was 7'4", defending the rim. And BLAM! Ron yoked it on three elite players plus caught the and-one as the crowd lost their sh*t.

In '85–'86, Ron Matthias averaged forty-one points a game at Palm Beach Junior

College to lead all NCAA scorers, but didn't finish his season due to disciplinary actions.

At the Entertainer's Basketball Classic at Rucker Park, Ron was known as "The Terminator," for good reason. He's *that* playground legend I saw with my own eyes who truly was good enough to not just be in the NBA but could've really done damage there.

And it's 1981, I'm watching Term eat up our competition at camp like hors d'oeuvres, and thinking in my head, *Dag, can I do that?*

I went back to the Goat with the skills I'd learned at camp. Inspired by Lincoln and Ron Matthias, I put some real thought toward changing how I approached the game. The daily routine became drills in the morning, light shoot-around early afternoon, run fulls at night when the old heads got out of work, then play 21, H.O.R.S.E., Around the World, or 5–2 as the park thinned out. In between, I was bumming a bite of someone's pizza crust and downing a pint-sized Tropicana OJ with a banana. I'd heard the fruit's potassium and magnesium would help prevent my muscles from cramping at night. Oh man, that was the worst. My calves would lock up for minutes until someone pushed my toes backward. I had no clue that I was completely dehydrated all the time. The water out the fountain at the park sometimes worked, most times nah. If there was an open fire hydrant, we would drink while getting our faces splashed and it'd be super-fresh cold. Bottled water not being a thing then, and even if it had been, I didn't have funds for that. By the end of each day, I'd have dried-up salt all over my face. Literally. But nothing was taking me away from being inside that fence. Nothing. Gone were the days of watching TV, being interested in dating girls, and playing any other sports. My singular focus was ball. That's it. And how beautiful that was!

This friendly dude named Pete started showing up to the Goat, and we took a liking to shooting jumpers together. His form was mega–textbook perfect, rotation lovely, and the ball always bounced right back to him, just like how Mario Elie had told me and Alix it should. He was six feet tall, and I had a feeling he might've played somewhere, but he was type humble with it and unassuming, so I didn't ask him anything. We were just present in the moment and enjoying being in the park.

One day, Pete showed up wearing Carolina-blue shorts. I looked at the pant leg and saw the Tar Heels logo. Back then, one couldn't just buy team merchandise at the local sporting goods shop. You had to earn that. So, I asked him how he'd gotten the jazzy gear, and he explained that he was on the staff at Dean Smith's summer camp, as in ACC legend Dean Smith, who had retired as the winningest coach in college basketball history.

Courtesy of Pete Strickland

Hold up. What?!

Turned out Pete, whose last name was Strickland, was First Team All-State in Maryland plus First Team All-WCAC, while directing DeMatha HS to a city title, DMV Catholic League title, and an eighth-place finish in the 1975 year-end US rankings. He had ended his college career as the all-time assist leader at D1 University of Pittsburgh. Pete had also played pro for a season in Ireland and created a b-ball frenzy in a country where Gaelic football and hurling ruled.

"Would you like me to teach you how to shoot a quick-release jump shot, Bobby?"

"Does a bear sh*t in the woods, Pete? Hello? Let's GO!"

Pete took the time to explain to an eager fourteen-year-old the foundation of form: "The elbow should be in line with the knee and parallel to the ground. The forearm should create an L, slightly less than a ninety-degree angle, so comfortable. Start at the triple-threat position with your knees bent, raise the ball up, then lift for the shot, releasing the ball at the height of your jump in one motion toward the rim, as if you were shooting out of a phone booth or giant tube, instead of throwing a dart at the wall . . ."

His words were jewels of advice, none of which I took lightly. Whether Pete was at the Goat or not, I heard his voice in my head, and followed suit. Repetition. Practice. Move to the open spot. Pull up off the dribble. Apply it in a game with D. Same thing the next day. My jumper was getting blocked less and less. Instead of shooting at the rim, I was releasing the ball with arc over outstretched hands. I was seeing results. And loving the feeling. *Loving*. I was no longer just playing aimlessly for fun. I became a threat.

Pete lived down the block from the Goat, so whether he was there to join me, or just walking home from the theater, the point god couldn't help seeing my earnest effort. Toward the end of the summer, he invited me to his crib. "I got something for you, Bobby." I knocked on his door, and his roommate opened it. She . . . was . . . drop-dead gorgeous. I tried my best not to stare as I stumbled to put words together. "Um . . . is Pete? I mean, is . . . Pete around?" My jump-shot buddy popped out and said, "I think you should have these," then blessed me with his UNC camp shorts. I felt like he'd just gave me a thousand-dollar bill. But then he handed me something that was priceless . . .

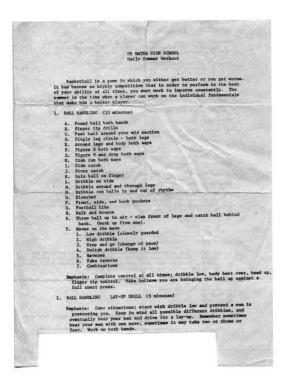

DE MATHA HIGH SCHOOL
Daily Summer Workout

Basketball is a game in which you either get better or you get worse. It has become so highly competitive that in order to perform to the best of your ability at all times, you must work to improve constantly. The summer is the time when a player can work on the individual fundamentals that make him a better player.

1. BALL HANDLING  (15 minutes)

   A.  Pound ball both hands
   B.  Finger tip drills
   C.  Pass ball around your mid section
   D.  Single leg circle - both legs
   E.  Around legs and body both ways
   F.  Figure 8 both ways
   G.  Figure 8 and drop both ways
   H.  Crab run both ways
   I.  Side catch
   J.  Front catch
   K.  Spin ball on finger
   L.  Dribble on side
   M.  Dribble around and through legs
   N.  Dribble two balls in and out of rhythm
   O.  Ricochet
   P.  Front, side, and back pockets
   Q.  Football hike
   R.  Walk and bounce
   S.  Throw ball up in air - slap front of legs and catch ball behind back. (work up from one).
   T.  Moves on the move
       1.  Low dribble (closely guarded
       2.  High dribble
       3.  Step and go (change of pace)
       4.  Switch dribble (keep it low)
       5.  Reverse
       6.  Fake reverse
       7.  Combinations

   Emphasis:  Complete control at all times; dribble low, body bent over, head up, finger tip control.  Make believe you are bringing the ball up against a full court press.

2. BALL HANDLING   LAY-UP DRILL  (5 minutes)

   Emphasis:  Game situations; start with dribble low and pretend a man is pressuring you.  Keep in mind all possible different dribbles, and eventually beat your man and drive for a lay-up.  Remember sometimes beat your man with one move; sometimes it may take two or three or four.  Work on both hands.

Pete Strickland played at DeMatha for Morgan Wootten, who retired in 2002 as the most successful coach in high school history with five national championships, 1,274 Ws, and a dozen players in the NBA. Wootten also won the 2000 Naismith Scholastic Coach of the Century award. Six years after graduating, Pete still had his mentor's summer workout sheet. And he passed it down to me. Like, that was the greatest assist I could've ever received. I felt like I was being gifted Naismith's original handwritten thirteen rules of basketball from December 21, 1891, the day the sport was born.

The drills listed were like nothing I'd ever seen, but the sheet was so much more than that. On the bottom was a mantra to live by, one that I already had in development from the example of Earl Manigault, but worded in a way that had clarity:

*Mr. Meant-To has a comrade and his name is Didn't-Do.*
*Have you ever chanced to meet them? Have they ever called on you?*
*These two fellows live together in the House-of-Never-Win.*
*And I am told that it is haunted by the Ghost of Might-Have-Been.*

I cut these words out and taped them on my bedroom wall by my pillow. I sought to be an overachiever. Pete Strickland was a six-foot white guy who was not dunking, but still played pro overseas and had an illustrious career because he could pass, shoot, and lead a team. He knew the game. He loved the sport. I identified with Pete's passion, and he joined the ranks of Gerald Erasme as players who I wanted to emulate. After being teammates with Richie Simmonds and Ron Matthias that summer, I knew I was not NBA material, in fact far from it, but that didn't mean I couldn't dream of making a life out of having a rock in my hand. My goal became clear.

I was already nutso about basketball, but with Wootten's bible, I went OD. If I visited my aunt in El Barrio, I had my ball with me to practice my form on her couch. When I went to the BX to visit my other aunt, I did ballhandling drills on the D train if the car was empty enough. My hand speed was improving. Every second that I was putting in, I was getting back.

The most profound advice that Wootten's summer workout sheet included was, "Remember, sometimes beat your man with one move; sometimes it may take two or three or four. Work on both hands." Every incentive I had to be creative up until this point had been from the street, yet here was a legend of the organized coaching ranks encouraging me to think out the box. Perhaps that was my own interpretation, I'll never know. Regardless, I was becoming a much improved ballplayer, rapidly.

The summer was ending, so I set a goal to beat three people I had never won a game against. The stage had to be at the Goat. First up was my pops, who was forty-six and not in tip-top shape. Nonetheless, Dad was more than three times my age with b-ball wisdom and had the Walt Frazier jumper that was hard to block, so I needed to go hard. W. He was happy for me, kind soul he was.

Next up was my oldest brother, Ray, who had eight years on me, was the strongest of the siblings, and the most skilled offensively. He was twenty-three and hadn't been playing much anymore, but it was still a battle. He'd lean into me to draw the foul, but we didn't play and-ones so if he called and the ball went in, it didn't count. Not sure I would've won if we were under the whistle, but in this park battle I took him out. Honestly, I simply used what he had taught me, and what I had watched him do to defenders for years. Ray was tight in the face afterward. Tight. I was his "little bruh-duh." He wasn't ready to accept that I had become a better player than him.

Last up was Lincoln Parker. Oh man. Bolo rock. The last we had spoken, he left me with the jewel that I needed the eye of the tiger. I still didn't truly have it, but what I did develop that he hadn't seen yet was a better jumper, improved ballhandling, and an increasing sense of defense. Linc was a ballplayer with fight in him, plus was an excellent football player, so he was very capable of playing rough if it meant securing a win. Some cats at the park thought he was a butcher. He fouled me hard on a couple of possessions, but not with any intention to hurt me. Never that. Lincoln was that older-brother figure who gave tough love when needed. We went back and forth, trading buckets, and he wound up with point. He missed the game winner, though. I got the rebound, took it back behind the line, and scored quickly before he could run up to defend the shot. "Point up."

"Win by two, Bobby."

After seeing how my brother Ray reacted to losing to me, I suddenly had doubt about the value of beating Lincoln, if I could. Did winning really matter to me? What was I trying to prove, or gain? Whatever the outcome, this was a learning experience. Everything I had practiced that whole summer was pouring out. I was seeing the value of hard work in real time.

Linc and I were both getting tired, as neither of us expected a contest as close as it had become. Then the light bulb went off in my head . . . *Remember, sometimes beat your man with one move; sometimes it may take two or three or four.*

Wootten's words of wisdom worked.

"Point game, Linc."

Next possession . . .

"Good game, Linc . . ."

I was exploding with joy, as well as shock, inside. I had beaten Lincoln Parker one-on-one. Just months prior he'd beaten me and a few other cats in a game of 21, where all of us were left on our donut. My French pastries were baked just right on this day, though. Didn't know if I could ever repeat the feat against him, and it didn't matter.

"Run it . . ."

I really didn't want to play again, but that's rude to win and then break out without giving the opponent a chance to get even. So, we ran it back. Lincoln rocked me. I had no chance the second go-round. All good.

"You got better, kid . . ."

It meant a lot to hear that from him. *A lot.*

That evening, the old heads came out after five p.m. to run fulls, as they always did. "Cookie Puss" Tim rubbed my boy's layup on the board. Pah-kang! Tim ran down the court with his shoulders hunched forward like a b-boy, then stuck his two thumbs up in front of his stomach while swinging them left to right, like a victory dance almost. My squad came back down, and in my head, I was like, *Nah, b, you not gonna do my mans like that*, and I went right at Tim in the paint. Naturally, he jumped to punch my sh*t, but since I had drawn him out of position, I dipped the ball down under his arm and dished a perfect dime.

"Soul food!" Tim gave me immediate props and started laughing. "I'm gonna start calling you 'Soul Food.'"

In one summer, I went from being a burger on my donut, to transforming into fluffy French pastries, and then ending fortified as Soul Food. I had earned my first tournament shirts, camp shorts, and nickname. I was making progress, paso a paso.

The fall of 1981 hit, and I was back at Brooklyn Tech for my sophomore year. Between my brothers' hand-me-down tournament shirts and the ones I'd earned during the summer, I dressed like a ballplayer every day of the week with the hopes my hard-rock classmates would cut me some slack and not jump me again—but I still got tested. One day in the cafeteria, I was innocently eating my thirty-five-cent ice-cream sandwich when two cats started sizing me up. EJ was the best player on varsity since NC State–bound forward Lorenzo Charles had graduated the year prior, and I had no idea how, but I was on his radar. "Chill, he's gonna be on the squad this year. He with me . . ." And just like how James Alston saved my ass freshman year, EJ blessed me with protective grace. The two dudes nodded and left me alone.

"Good lookin' out, EJ!"

"Don't worry about it. Stay ready for tryouts. They coming up soon . . ."

With six thousand kids at Tech, there was a huge pool of talent. I felt confident I could at least make JV, though. I had stopped cutting class and was a grade-A student again, so there were no eligibility issues standing in my way. I got way better over the summer and was really looking forward to seeing what I could do.

During a gym class, our teacher took us outside on a cold day to run laps around the building. Since I wasn't the fastest cat in the world, I took this as prep for getting in shape and went hard. One classmate lagged way behind, and we waited for him to come around the corner before going back inside. He finally showed up, but now in a white T-shirt, and was crying. Some kids had burped him for his leather bomber. The constant threat of getting vicked or jumped for no reason was wack to me. I felt bad for homeboy. I deliberately never wore anything of monetary value that would attract a stickup crew, and hated that I had to constantly think two steps ahead. That was the

Courtesy of Danny Perry

**00 47**

eighties, though. I loved everything else about New York Sh*tty, so I dealt with it. We all did.

On the first day of tryouts, I had a plan: Go hard every drill. Dive for loose balls. Encourage my teammates. I wasn't gonna outmuscle or outjump anyone, but I knew I could display mental toughness and extra effort, like the message on Ronnie Ryer's Wichita State shorts. Well, at least the latter part.

It seemed like there were two hundred students on that first day. Two stuck out: Kyle Rhoden, a lefty guard with a nice handle and a T-shirt that had his nickname, Ice Cube, in iron-on letters; and Mike Drake, a skinny 6'8" freshman who was reppin' a Holcombe Rucker Memorial T-shirt just like me. We all got cool and kept giving each other a pound to show support. The three of us got invited back the next day.

With 75 percent of the first day's group sliced, the comp on the second day of tryouts got a lot stiffer, with dudes fighting for spots on either varsity or JV. When we scrimmaged, Kyle was on an opposing squad, and on one play, he V-dribbled behind his back three times in a row. I smiled inside, like, *He got the vicious style!* Point guards in organized ball back then were expected to get the rock across half-court, then dump it into the post. No showboating allowed. That play probably cost him joining the upperclassmen like EJ, but Kyle sent out the bat signal to those who cared, like, *Yeah, b, I got a handle.*

Kyle's move made me realize that I hadn't done anything yet to get noticed, so a few plays later, I chased down a breakaway. I had seen all-American guard John Paxson at Notre Dame run right in front of an offensive player—like literally cut off their path to the cup—in order to knock the ball out of his hands. I did the same exact thing and got a carbon-copy result. Brooklyn Tech's coach was Mr. McMurrow, who had a gentle presence unlike some of the a\*\*holes on the sidelines who lead our youth. "Good D!" he shouted.

For the final drill, McMurrow put Mike Drake on one end, and everyone else took turns dribbling from half-court to try and score on him. Mike was swatting shots like batting practice with a wiffle ball, as in, *This is easy*. I thought about coach Wootten's wise words: . . . *beat your man with one move; sometimes it may take two or three or four*, and with all eyes in the gym on me, I faked Mike with a stutter step, then scored. Luckily. I wasn't used to being guarded by someone that tall.

The next day, I checked to see if I'd made JV, and was amped to see my name. I reported to the first practice that afternoon, only to notice Coach walk into the gym with a long face. "Congratulations, you've all made the team," he shared. "Unfortunately, the PSAL has withdrawn funding for our junior varsity this season . . . You can play today, but this will be the last practice unless you're on varsity. Really sorry, fellas . . ."

I was done with Tech after that day. Between the constant threat of violence and then the b-ball rug being pulled out from under me, I had no interest in finishing my high school days there.

I was boys with Darryl Roberts from around my way who attended the Canterbury boarding school in Connecticut. Darryl was an uber-positive dude and compassionate friend, always making the best of any situation he was put in. We'd play ball together when he was home, then we'd write goofy letters to each other throughout the school year. When I told him about what had happened, he introduced me to the ABC program, which stood for A Better Chance. The nonprofit helped place gifted inner-city students of color into learning environments that could potentially improve their ability to reach higher education. That's how D got out of New York. I hoped for the same and applied.

I was so hungry for b-ball. I wanted to eat, sh\*t, sleep the game. I dreamed about playing, whether asleep or lost in thought on the forty-five-minute train ride back and forth to Tech every day. I imagined moves, replayed highlights in my head of players I'd seen, and would even doodle court action during class when it'd get boring. I just couldn't get enough. I started searching high and low for any b-ball-related info to read. Most print coverage would be about the NBA, so it'd be delicious to find books about my world—the asphalt—like *The City Game* by Pete Axthelm, *The Basketball Diaries* by Jim Carroll, Rick Telander's excellent *Heaven Is a Playground,* and the epic *In-Your-Face Basketball Book* where authors Alexander Wolff and Chuck Wielgus Jr. traveled across the US and wrote reviews of every court they played at. I was barely getting out of the Upper West Side to play, and these dudes went cross-country searching for pickup?! That seemed like an unthinkable holy grail. *If only one day,* I thought.

I could catch a televised college or NBA game on the weekends, but if someone did a freak pass or move, most times the announcers wouldn't even acknowledge it, and the network wouldn't show a replay. They were numb to what the hood loved seeing. Local TV sportscaster Warner Wolf would share a few seconds of exciting highlights during his segment on the nightly news, though. I'd always look forward to him saying, "Let's go to the videotape!" It was all just a tease and never enough, which in a way was a good thing. Those of us who loved b-ball like nobody's business had to either imagine it, pass down folklore, or be there in the moment. The fear of missing out was ridiculous.

Watching players on TV was crazy different than peeping them up close and personal in the summer Pro-Am at Xavier HS. Entry was free, and I could stand a few feet from the baseline. Gus Williams aka "The Wizard" of the Seattle Supersonics led all scorers in the 1979 NBA Finals with 28.6 ppg, yet he'd go just as hard against the city's best. Cleveland Cavs PG Geoff Huston from Brownsville, Brooklyn, dropped sixty-one that night. Future NBA champ Wes Matthews Sr. would be catching dunks at 6'1" and was quicker than ramen noodles, but the player who amazed me the most was Nancy Lieberman. The 1976 Olympic silver medalist and two-time national College Player of the Year moved so fluidly, with or without the ball. Her midrange was wet paint. She was the first woman to play in the Rucker Pro League men's division, and in 1983 became the first woman to try out for an NBA team. Seeing her and all the other Pro-Am talent was mystifying, as well as inspiring.

Could only read and watch but so much. Ultimately, the whole point was to be out there playing. I was able to enter a couple of tournaments as '81 transitioned into '82, including the Boys Harbor on 104th. The gym doubled as the rehearsal space for the Big Apple Circus and their animals, so the wood floor didn't exactly smell like flowers. Our best player was a fellow Boricua who was also on the All Hallows HS squad. There was always a sprinkling of Puerto Rican players in every league I was in, but it was rare to see two of us on the court at the same time, much less starting in the backcourt together. I enjoyed playing with him; there was an unspoken cultural comfort. The lefty guard wore low-cut Converse Dr. Js with a light-blue chevron and stripe, too. He was cool as sh*t—nobody had those.

I joined the Central Baptist Kings, and we played in a few tournaments that winter/spring, including City-Wide at Brandeis HS where we got waxed, but also the PAL deep in the LES at the Henry Street Settlement. Our first game there, we took the F to Delancey Street, and the toughest kid on our squad stopped us before we even left the train station platform. "I'm from Harlem so I ain't no punk," he shared with a straight face, "but chyo, we in the Lower now. Tuck your chains, lace your sneakers, watch each other's back, and be aware. If any one of us gets jumped, we all meet back here after the game on the uptown side . . ."

Delancey Street had a rep for stickup kids. Some of the best sneaker shops in the city were down there, and credit cards were nonexistent for us teenagers, so all purchases were cash only. The vultures were fully aware of that, too. Cats would either get stuck for their stack of singles or for their brand-new Puma Clydes walking back to the subway entrance. Pick your poison.

Our team captain had our guard up so high that somehow whenever we played down there, we had the X-ray goggles on and rocked. We wound up taking second place, and in one game I recorded my first career blocked shot. I studied how 1981 NCAA final MVP Isiah Thomas of Indiana University used to defend jump shots. The six-foot PG would leap to the side of the shooter instead of the front, and would get the block where the player cocked it back before releasing. Employing this method, I shocked a PAL opponent—and my own teammates for that matter—by punching a fifteen-footer then going the opposite direction for the breakaway buttercup.

Spring 1982 arrived, and although I'd missed out on an entire season of playing high school ball, I was grateful for the number of opportunities my city still provided me to rock. With summer a few months away, I was feeling positive. That energy served me well, as I got a letter of acceptance to the ABC program. Couldn't have been better timing. Tech had a rule that no student could graduate without passing swimming class. The test was to simply swim the entire length of the pool. I couldn't do it yet, though. I had a fear of the water something terrible. I was always bullied around the waves as a kid. Family members would push me into the deep end, knowing full well I didn't know how to breath, stroke, or even float on my own. Then when I was eleven, my cousin Billy Clark drowned near the dock of a lake by his home in Jersey. He was the best swimmer in his county. I was shook. If he couldn't save himself, how could I?

Two semesters in a row I had doggy-paddled three-quarters of the way and then my lungs would shrink from fright until I reached for the edge to throw the towel in. I tried, and I could give myself grace knowing that this would be my last hurrah in that cold-ass pool. I would be heading out of the city the upcoming fall for my junior year thanks to ABC, but the real gratitude was for my boy Darryl Roberts, who'd put the battery in my backpack. One day we were at his cousin Lawana's crib at Westgate, and Darryl dead-ass was like, "Bobby, let's train for the Olympics, man. I think we can make it!" And for weeks leading into the summer, we took turns encouraging each other while doing toe raises, push-ups, and sit-ups out on her terrace. Like he truly had conviction we could qualify.

Seven years later, Darryl took that positive attitude all the way to the North Pole on an expedition called Icewalk '89, becoming the youngest US explorer to ever reach there, but more importantly the second Black person to ever see that part of the world. Halfway through the voyage, Darryl developed frostbite in his toe, and the team doctor determined he should turn back home. Darryl had trained for two years and was adamant about reaching his goal, even if he had to limp to the end. He returned to New York a hero and was even featured on the cover of the *New York Daily News*.

There was a saying in Spanish my mother taught me as a kid, *Dime con quién tú andas, y te diré quién tú eres,* which translated into, *Tell me who you walk with, and I'll tell you who you are.* I knew exactly why I gravitated toward Darryl's friendship in 1982: he inspired me. What he saw in me I wasn't really sure of, though. I didn't have the self-esteem or confidence that he possessed to warrant him wanting to "walk" with me.

Or did I? Was my passion for basketball transforming my character in a manner I wasn't aware of yet?

One thing for sure was that I was finished with Brooklyn Tech. I had willed that into existence. Realizing my mindful powers was forthcoming . . .

**SINCE 1982**

# FRANKFURTERS

## ON THE BEATBOX

I rejoined Central Baptist for the summer of 1982 to play in the Holcombe Rucker and also RYA, which was a cool tournament tucked behind the old Polo Grounds site. We had a crazy coach named Al who loved getting exasperated when we turned the ball over or lost, but would then joke around with us after each game either way. Our main play was "Ice Cream!" which wasn't much of a strategy at all. The starting point guard would get an iso and the rest of us would clear out. He'd call it out every few possessions, which meant I really didn't touch the ball much.

I wasn't the team captain or best player, so when the director of the Central Baptist Kings program, Pastor Don, asked if I could coach the biddies squad for kids three or four years younger than me, I was kind of shocked. I was only fifteen. Pastor Don had watched me at their camp the summer before, saw my improvement in the winter leagues, and honored my dedication by sometimes opening up the basement gym so I could practice on my own when it was too brick outside. I had also played piano at his church, so he took a liking to me. Was I qualified to lead a group of snot-nosed preteens? Hell nah! I dug the challenge, though, and accepted. In the least, I'd have access to an indoor court when it was raining or OD hot outside, so I had selfish motives.

Fortunately for me, not many kids showed up to tryouts. I didn't have the heart to cut anybody, knowing how wack that felt myself. And perhaps even more fortuitously, the players who comprised the main nucleus were all legit competitors for their age group already, so it wasn't gonna be a case of the blind leading the blind. Gary Bien-Aime aka "Gary Gnu" was a workhorse with a great attitude. I taught him how to beat a double team by dribbling the ball first behind his back to lure one defender to reach, then going under his legs to split the two opponents, and "Big Face Gary" completely ran with the instruction and made it his signature move. That made me happy. Craig Batchelor was a straight scorer with a variety of runners, pop-ups, and lefty lays. "Craig Batch" went on to be a key component in La Salle Academy's winning season on a national level in 1989. I couldn't take credit for that one bit, but it still made me proud.

My two favorite players to coach on that biddie squad were Carlos Arias and Mike Parker, Lincoln Parker's younger brother. Los and Mike were best friends, inseparable like conjoined twins, goofy as sh*t, and completely lovable. I started inviting them to my seven a.m. morning workouts at the Goat to teach them drills, where I discovered that by going over mechanics with someone else, I was able to break down fundamentals in a manner that became beneficial to me, too. I was learning by teaching, similar to the Montessori ideology. Brilliant.

One hot evening, the three of us were going hard, sweating, and we got hungry. I told them I had discovered that the key to improving was . . . eating frankfurters. They were gullible, so I led them on. "Yeah, man, eat frankfurters for breakfast tomorrow," as they nodded. "Eat frankfurters for lunch, then dinner, too. Every day. Frankfurters! See how nice your handle gets . . ." They looked at each other suspiciously but were both too young to doubt, so Carlito blurted, "Okay, Bob, frankfurters it is. We on it!" at which point I cracked up and was like, "Yo, I'm totally joking." All three of us were rolling.

Carlos became a skilled offensive player at Proctor Academy in New Hampshire. Mike lit up future 1989 HS Player of the Year Kenny Anderson for forty points in a game at Stone Gym, which was unheard of in an era where Kenny was considered the greatest player in the history of NYC high school basketball. Mike "Butters" went on to destroy private school comp at McBurney with twenty-five-plus ppg, then finished his collegiate career as Cornell's all-time steals leader.

Both Mike and Los accomplished all this without eating frankfurters, so I couldn't put a feather in my cap for any of it, but the experience of coaching them taught me something extremely valuable—that I had a way with young people. Growing up, I was the little one always getting bullied by older cats. Sh*t rolls downhill, right? I didn't buy into that. I wanted to treat others how I would want to be treated. I didn't perpetuate abuse or tough love for that matter, and excuse the behavior with, *Well, I got it bad, so let me inflict this pain onto the next person.* Nah, and especially not in the precious realm of basketball.

The other key takeaway was that it was possible to learn the game while having fun. I was used to coaches putting pressure on kids to use ball to get out of the hood by earning an athletic scholarship or eventually going pro. I understood the advantage of having a competitive edge, and that worked wonderfully for many, but that wasn't *my* reality. Of course, I could benefit from setting a high goal like playing overseas, but couldn't I gain just as much from the transcendental mind state that playing, practicing, teaching, and learning took me to? In these instances, the escape was temporary, though still impactful. I didn't have the language as a fifteen-year-old kid, but I was arriving at the notion of basketball mindfulness. Being present in the moment, and finding my peace and joy right there, on the court.

Or off it. The glass entrance at Westgate was practically the size of two Macy's store windows, and became my outside rehearsal space. Similar to a ballerina in a studio using the wall-to-wall mirrors to perfect a move, I was transfixed anytime I would dribble while staring at myself in the reflection. The penalty for losing my control was either chasing the rock out into the oncoming traffic or sprinting forward to avoid my Spalding cracking one of the two major panes. There was an awning above, so I was waterproof, too.

Dribbling by myself was blissful. I heard that Hall of Famer "Pistol" Pete Maravich would dribble in the aisle of his hometown's theater while catching a flick, and 1981 NBA champion Nate "Tiny" Archibald used to pat his rock walking to the bodega every day to catch groceries. Both of these guards had legendary handles, and I was inspired by their work ethic. I would try to see if I could walk our entire block from Columbus to Amsterdam bouncing between my legs continuously without looking down. Keeping my head up was how I'd see an open teammate, or a defender trying to blindside me to take my cookies. I'd nod to one of my neighbors walking by, but otherwise I'd zone the f out. The sound of rubber hitting the concrete sidewalk every two seconds had a rhythm which was soothing and required concentration. The experience was actually musical.

The Big Apple Games had tryouts at Brandeis HS. Even though the majority of players were incoming seniors, I somehow made the cut and we played against squads from every borough up at Kennedy HS in the Bronx. That was the best team I'd played on up to that point, and not to take away from the talent, but our coach, Vaughn, was the main reason in my eyes. He had thunder thighs, so when he'd have us sit against the wall with no chair underneath until our legs trembled and some dudes would be screaming, "How much more time until two minutes?" I knew the pain was worth it if it meant I'd get bop like he had.

Vaughn noticed I enjoyed dribbling drills before and after practice, so he started expanding my regimen. He had me do V dribbles behind my back while doing defensive slides left to right at the same time, which helped me push off my foot more effectively to make the move more believable. He challenged me to do each move repeatedly the full length of the court and back. Behind the back continuously while running full speed with no collect-yourself dribble in between for ninety-four feet was another task. My mind was blown. The possibilities for combos were endless. The Big Apple Games went by quickly, but the impact of Coach Vaughn on my outlook was monumental. He was the first trainer who really believed I could develop a freak handle. He made me feel seen.

When I joined the Upward Fund Summer Academy in El Barrio, my outlook on life really took an upswing. The nonprofit was committed to teaching academic and career skills, using basketball as a draw. The free weekday camp went from nine a.m. to five p.m. for eight weeks, with a hundred campers using the PS 96 indoor gym and schoolyard. Director Gene Kitt and Coach Mike Brown had us learn fundamentals in the morning, then we'd run halves or fullies in the afternoon. In between, we learned how to write a résumé, make a ten-year projection, and even partake in mock job interviews with real-deal employers. The UF educators would provide feedback on what we needed to improve on.

Another feature at the Upward Fund that I wasn't getting otherwise was the program's weekly invited speakers. Most of these guests would kick the cliché, "You can do anything you put your mind to . . ." to which I'd reply in my head, *Stop gassing us up*. Not in the US at least, where systematic racism, stereotyping, prejudice, classism, sexism, homophobia, ageism, ableism, white patriarchy, ignorance, and the very exploitative nature of capitalism kept too many heads in my community down. I saw too many Black and Brown college graduates come home with degrees who still could not find decent jobs. There was no true meritocracy. The success stories were a minority, and at times served to placate the masses from feeling ripped off.

Iona University star guard Tony Hargraves came through and kept it the realest. Tony didn't try to sell us dreams. Instead, he really drove home the point that hard work was the key to giving yourself a chance in life. If a door did wind up opening, you owed it to yourself to be ready for it. I interpreted what he was sharing as I should be best prepared for whatever opportunities came my way. If they didn't work out, wasn't going to be because I hadn't given it my best. Shots I pass on will never go in.

The beauty of the Upward Fund was that the atmosphere was far from just serious life lessons and career skills. I was having a blast making new friends, particularly with Mark Pearson, John Merz, and Ted Lake. I had first seen Mark while playing pickup at Central Park months prior. The 6'5" swingman from Brooklyn had a sweet jumper and a smooth in-and-out dribble which was his go-to move. When he left 86th Street that day, he grabbed his Riverside Church bag, which was the official stamp of hood credibility, and walked off in New Balance 480 nubuck high-tops, which I hadn't seen anyone else wearing yet. Strong first impression!

John Merz was a carbon copy of Pistol Pete's game trapped in a body made of angel hair noodles. I *loved* watching "Johnny Snakeback" play. His jump shot was correctly aligned. His two-hand chest pass was mega textbook. He had a fundamentally sound game mixed with boogie and flair. John and I also bonded when we opened up about both of our fathers being alcoholics. Other than my siblings, I had never gotten close to anyone who knew what it was like to see their parent stumbling then falling on the sidewalk in broad daylight while pedestrians were walking by. That happened to me while I was working my first job at Alicia's as a delivery boy in 1980, literally outside the storefront window when I was packing groceries for a customer. The owner, Miguel, was a kind man, and nodded to me that it was

okay to step out and help my dad back up on his feet then take him home. The whole experience was embarrassing. John was my first buddy who got it. He'd been through the same.

Ted Lake was younger than me in age yet at the same time way older than me in street knowledge. He lived a few blocks from the Fund in the Taft projects and had the Harlem b-ball aesthetic down pat as well as a hip hop cultural edge to him to the fullest. When Ted dropped fifty in the Holcombe Rucker Memorial on eventual champs the TS Bucks, he earned

the nickname Ted "Nitro." The lefty had the diddy bop, gear, slang, and a stutter-step move with dip sauce for two that was pure.

Mark and John were no strangers to hip hop, either. Mark wrote SAKE and was tagging the ding-dong lines with seventies legend TRIKE 1, both in the yards and the insides while riding the iron horse. John didn't bomb trains; he just knew what time it was. The live recording of "Flash Is on the Beatbox" was kind of the litmus test to know who was down by law and not, cuz similar to the Treacherous Three's "The Body Rock,"

Courtesy of Mark Pearson

you just weren't going to hear that joint on the radio. You had to be *inside* the culture, *living* the culture, to be up on it. When Mark, John, Ted, and I all shared the lyrics, "*For all you MCs in a crew, this is what we want you to do . . . Shoo, shoo, shoo, shoo, shoo . . .*" we looked at each other in a unifying way. Four dudes from different neighborhoods and backgrounds, bonding over ball, kicks, and beats in what felt like a secret society.

Almost daily after the Upward Fund was over, the four of us would head to Mickey D's to bug out. Some days we'd ask for one order of french fries to split between us, with a side order of courtesy water—"Four cups, please." We'd yap for an hour about whatever Peter Vecsey had written in the *New York Post*. Vecsey and "Butch" Purcell were the legendary coaches of the Westsiders and were responsible for bringing Julius Erving up to Rucker Park in 1971 when nooobody knew who the future Hall of Famer was (outside of UMass fans who had seen him dominate untelevised college games there for three years).

**FRANKFURTERS ON THE BEATBOX**

Vecsey's eye for talent was just as sharp as his lip, or typewriter, and he'd fillet pro players in the *Post*. He was the first newspaper columnist completely dedicated to NBA editorial we knew of, which was a treat in 1982 when coverage of the league was thin. Mark, John, Ted, and I would laugh out loud or get completely upset at some of the insane claims he'd make about our favorite players. Readers either loved or hated Pete, but his commentary was no different than how closely we critiqued people's games, so he felt like one of us.

Like we'd frown upon point guards who were one-hand bandits, dribbling up the left side of the court with their right hand. Yuck. That described more than half of the league's top stars. Dribbling with your body between the ball and the defender was a no-no as well, other than a spin move. We all thought strongly that the true New York way was to pat that rock right in front of the D. If your handle was nice enough, you'd bait your man to reach and wouldn't get ripped.

Ted, who was a fantastic storyteller, explained how Leroy Shaw did the ultimate disrespect at the LaGuardia House Tournament on 116th. "La Luscious Lee" got picked up full-court and proceeded with V dribbles behind his back . . . with his back to the defender! Like saying, *You suck. I don't even have to face you and you still not gonna take my cookies, b.* John was also mystified by Shaw's whip-whop when the point god came down on a two-on-one fast break at the 1982 Pro-Am downtown, put the ball behind his back as if he was passing to his teammate, then proceeded to bounce the rock in front of his body back to his right hand. Leroy's defender completely bit the fake, and La Luscious drove to the hole K-Solo untouched for the two-piece. A third of a second later, eight hundred people in the stands went bananas as John's dome piece exploded. It's the same trick Kobe did sixteen years later in his first All-Star Game when the announcer screamed, "I'm not sure I've ever seen that move before!" and all of us in New York were like, "Props to Kobe, but the dude on the mic needs to come around the way . . ."

Ted also told us about the time Joe Hammond showed up for a game at LaGuardia. Word spread around Harlem, and before tip-off the small gym got so packed the sidelines were no longer visible. They were overshadowed by bodies. The legend, who held the record for most points in a Rucker Pro game with seventy-four, proceeded to drop fifteen in the first two minutes, all on bank shots. That's a lot of buckets with no three-point line, but the truly uncanny factor was that the backboards were half-moon there. Ted told us that cats were so amazed, they started breathing too heavy, and with the heat in the room, the game got canceled due to the condensation level. "The Destroyer" might've had one hundred in that match had they not stopped. Who knows . . .

There was so much history that wasn't being documented, only being passed on by word of mouth, generation to generation. Maybe, just maybe, the playground folklore got a little exaggerated as it aged, but who cared? The stories were fantastical. I was bright-eyed and loved soaking it all in.

Bonding with Mark, John, and Ted the summer of '82 gave me a firm grip on my identity as a New York ballplayer, which could not have been better timed considering I was about to go away to school come September. I still had a week left in me before I packed my bags. Hitting West 4th had been on the bucket list ever since I'd seen the opening scene of the 1979 movie *Fastbreak* starring all-time NYC legend Bernard King, so I trekked downtown to the mecca of pickup. I had third next, waited over an hour to get on cuz dudes just kept arguing and arguing, almost as if it was theater for the audience on the fence, and then my squad lost.

Uptown had the b-ball inteligencia on lock, the most knowledgeable crowd possible. The Vil had the opposite, from NYU students, jazz-club hangovers, a strong gay community, off-Broadway actors, handball hustlers, fashion models en route to go-sees, and all types of characters walking up and down Sixth Avenue, all of whom would stop to see who was running. I dug the experience of playing in front of random folks watching. With the train station exit for the A, B, C, D, E, and F leading directly to the fenced entrance of the court, it was a no-brainer why every ballplayer in the city, or the world for that matter, would want to show out there.

I hadn't spent much time at the Goat that whole summer, so I had to pay homage to my personal sanctuary before jetting to school. As always, the tall old man who wore a kufi and never played was sitting on the bench watching. I never knew his name, but I always greeted him. Had no idea if he was nasty in his day, or just simply enjoyed being a spectator of the playground circuit. I played better when he was present, though. Maybe he was a college scout? Who knew? If this was an opportunity, I wanted to seize it.

As I was hitting jumpers in a game of 21, I realized Earl Manigault had been peeping me, too. Sometimes he'd lurk on the bench to drink a brew. Earl stepped toward the court and nodded at me. In his mystical way and with his infinite wisdom, he then said in his gravelly voice, "Nice jumper." My heart rate jumped thirty beats per minute. Wait. What? The Goat, one of my heroes, thought I had a nice jump shot? And shared that unsolicited?

I held on to that compliment like Silver Surfer would his cosmic board at the Pepsi Hot Shot Manhattan Qualifier down in Chelsea. Although the winners would get airtime during televised NBA games, and the competition was national, not that many heads showed up, and not anyone of note. We took turns shooting from five different spots. For me, it was like playing Around the World back at the Goat. I won, and got invited to return for the NYC championship, but the date was on the same week I was going to dip to school out of state, so I had to pass on it.

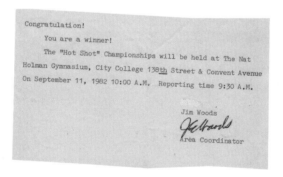

Congratulation!

You are a winner!

The "Hot Shot" Championships will be held at The Nat Holman Gymnasium, City College 138th Street & Convent Avenue On September 11, 1982 10:00 A.M. Reporting time 9:30 A.M.

Jim Woods
*JWoods*
Area Coordinator

The summer was over, and I was weeks away from turning sixteen. I had a jumper, a decent handle, friends who identified with my fever finally, and the stamp of approval from a venerated asphalt god. I didn't know what life was gonna be like at a sleepaway educational program, but I was ready for the next movement. At least I thought I was . . .

# THE OPTIMIST

In September 1982, I hopped on the Amtrak to Philadelphia, then transferred to the SEPTA Paoli line to finally arrive in the suburbs of Ardmore. ABC had placed me in the Lower Merion HS public school program for at-risk students who showed promise. I had hoped to be in a boarding school like Darryl Roberts, but failing seven classes my freshman year at Brooklyn Tech hindered that opportunity. At ABC-LM, I would live with nine other students, two guardians, plus two resident tutors in a big three-story house. The adults were there to keep us on track, just in case.

Directly across the street was "The Soul Shack," a community gym so small there wasn't even room for a half-court circle. I was amped regardless. I had a place to play when it rained that I wouldn't have to sneak into like Columbia. Right on the corner was an outdoor court that was real suburban, bordered with wood planks and grass, plus no cracks in the asphalt or shattered glass like I was used to. The first night sleeping at the ABC House, I looked down the block and was shocked as the sun started to set. I thought the huge lights were for the baseball field, but then . . . *bam* . . .

Lighted courts? Really? I literally thought, *Am I in heaven right now?* I had become accustomed to playing in the dark at the Goat, using the dim shine from the nearest lamppost or the moon's glow to illuminate the rim. I honestly felt that made me a better shooter. If I could hit jumpers while barely seeing the goal, how much easier would it be when I had clear vision?

I completely welcomed my new environment. Was a far cry from NY, in too many ways. The first week of classes, the finest student in the entire district made it known she liked me. Hold up. Me? The dude who has no gear, no hairstyle, and wears tournament shirts every day? I was used to getting absolutely no play from any girl I ever had a crush on, dating back to fourth grade when I first started getting that *Ooh-wee!* feeling in my heart around a classmate I found attractive.

The only date I had been on as a teenager was with a classmate at Brooklyn Tech. We hit the movies then she invited me back to her crib on Roosevelt Island, which was cool cuz I had never been on the tram before. Within minutes after arriving, someone banged on her door wild hard. Her next-door neighbor was also her jealous ex, and he was vexed. Great. She suggested I leave. As I exited the building, there were eight dudes in a semicircle waiting for me. Her bozo-clown boo stepped up and said, "Don't ever come back here again, ya heard?" I was like, "Cool, b, you got that." His boys bumped my shoulder and kicked my bag as I walked past, but otherwise let me go unscathed. Suffice to say, I never went out with her again.

So one day, the Pam Grier of Lower Merion HS pushed up and kissed me after school, and I had no clue how to react or follow up. I was completely shook, a virgin with no game, other than on the court. The short-lived moment was certainly a boost to my confidence.

Not everyone in Ardmore was as welcoming to me, though.

Chip Jones was slated to be a star guard at LM, but supposedly was dealing with some personal issues so didn't play. Naturally, I wanted to test where I stood talent-wise locally and would relish anytime we could go against each other on the Ardmore Avenue court. Philadelphia's version of NYC's 21 game was called Roughhouse, where there was still no teams, no teammates, but there were also no outs or fouls, which made the comp play, well, a lot rougher than what I was used to. Cats weren't vibing with my penchant for dribbling between my legs three times fast and low, and on one play after scoring, instead of Chip checking the ball up, he darted that sh*t projectile-speed at my face. Bang! I felt the grain of the rubber on my forehead and my face turned red from the impact. That was about all the reaction I had in me, though. Just like when the bully did the same to me at the Goat a year prior, I just hoped the situation wouldn't escalate, and I "turned the other cheek." The park was always my sanctuary, yet that didn't mean it was a safe space. Not back home, and not in my new one, either.

The school bus used to pick us up before seven a.m., and naturally some of the students were either half-asleep or awake and grumpy. Laribee Simms was a strong, sinewy 6'4" cat who always lurked in the backseats. One morning he blurted, "These young boys from New York be thinking they all that," while looking directly at me as I came on board. I had worn a different tournament shirt from back home for almost two weeks at that point. Although indeed they were badges of honor for me personally, sh*t, I'd worked hard to earn each of them; I wasn't trying to show off. I simply didn't have any other gear, and besides, the main thing I identified myself as was being a ballplayer. I wanted the world to recognize that. I certainly wasn't trying to stir up any trouble.

I didn't find Chip and Laribee nearly as intimidating as the student body at Lower Merion, which was predominantly white and affluent. There were juniors like me who would be dropped off at school in Mercedes-Benzes and Jaguars. There were seniors who drove up in their own whips. I would ride my brother's hand-me-down Raleigh ten-speed to the other side of the train tracks past Montgomery Avenue and see *Falcon Crest*–type homes with acres of manicured front lawns. The Main Line had so much wealth that our school facilities were even more state-of-the-art than some small colleges with large endowments I'd visited. I'd never seen this level of resources for education and sports. I didn't know if or where I fit in. I envisioned making varsity, but could I keep up academically? I was grappling with esteem issues.

November arrived. I made varsity and was expecting to get some burn, but when the football season ended weeks later, the starting quarterback, who was a great athlete, joined the squad and there went my anticipated minutes. These dudes had played together all their lives, and I was the new kid on the block. I was fine with earning my stripes, and committed to being the first to practice, last to leave, even if it meant missing the school bus back to the ABC House. I got into my routine of drills, both from Wootten and Vaughn, and the LM coach, Mike Manning, took notice: "Robert, you can do things with the ball that I've never seen before." There was a line in my favorite movie, *One on One*, where actor Robby Benson says, "That guy from New York . . . he's got moves I've never seen before!" and I recorded the audio of the dialogue onto an analog cassette so I could listen to it on repeat. Hearing those same words being said to me was surreal, like life imitating art. Coach continued, "Every Saturday, we do a free clinic for kids called the Ardmore Optimist. You should run the dribbling station . . ." I gladly accepted the second unsolicited offer to teach basketball within months of each other. Perhaps this was a calling, and I rolled with the rhythm.

Before our first game, Coach Manning passed out unis. I was on some New York–we-wear-our-gear-baggy sh*t, so even though I had late dibs on what number I could choose, I was amped that there was an XL #43 still available. That was the digits for Brooklyn Tech star Lorenzo Charles, who was playing for NC State that season. When Charles dunked a buzzer-beater to win the 1983 NCAA final, I lost my sh*t. I repped the four-three with much pride after that.

ROW 1—KNEELING—MARC TURNER, ANTHONY HORSHAW, ROBERT GARCIA, TIM SHAW, TOM KRUG.
BACK—ASST. COACH JOHN BYRNE, ERIC JONES, MIKE SIMMS, PETER BARTON, CHUCK SABATINI, PALMER YALE
JACK CUSKEY, MOALEY DINNAR, HEAD COACH MIKE MANNING.

Lower Merion HS had a storied b-ball tradition that I was proud to be a part of. My teammate Mark Brogan's older brother Jim was an alum playing in the NBA for the Clippers that season. The program also won the Pennsylvania state championship in 1933, '41, '42, and '43. Gregg Long from the class of '75 was *the* local legend in Ardmore and almost made the league when he tried out for the Bullets. Long would play pickup with us from time to time, and the 6'4" guard could put it up. Seeing how nice he was and knowing he still didn't make it was a reality check. Although the fantasy of competing at Madison Square Garden one day had long fizzled out, I still had my hopes on playing college ball. For inspiration, I used to read *Street and Smith's College Basketball Preview* cover to cover. I could tell you who the assistant coach and twelfth man on the bench were at over two hundred D1 schools. Yes, I was a nerd.

Photographer unknown

\* \* \*

Our '82–'83 season flew by, and coming back home to New York for spring break to catch the Wheelchair Classic with my buddy John Merz was a treat. Every top high school player in the city was selected. The gym was packed and rowdy, until "Pearl" Washington aka "Pac Man" out of Boys High walked in, then the crowd got hush. The all-American point god had on a black Gauchos jacket that he left open to show off the gold chains draped around his neck. He didn't *think* he was all that—Pearl purely *was*, and we were in awe.

As much as Washington was the talk of the town, the biggest *Ooh! Ah!* in that all-star game happened when a slow, large-bodied white guard did a low, unhurried crossover that made his defender slide two feet in the wrong direction. I couldn't even see if he made the bucket after the slick move because every single soul in the stands immediately stood up and screamed. I had gone a whole season at Lower Merion without seeing one highlight like I had just witnessed. Being back in New York juiced me up. The mental wiring for appreciating b-ball's nuances was upper-echelon. I didn't have height, hops, strength, or quickness, but if I could bring creativity and deception to the floor, maybe I could get attention from a college scout. In the least, I could crowd-please and get satisfaction off that.

The one person at Lower Merion who "got it" was my ABC House classmate Ahmad Hooper, who was two grades behind me. I took him under my wing like a little brother. Even though I was drifting from claiming Catholicism, I still enjoyed some of the jewels I'd catch from the sermons, one of which was that we should not be hesitant to tell our friends,

*I love you.* Even though we were silly teenagers, I went back to the crib and in front of all ten housemates, I told Ahmad those very three heartfelt words. Dudes burst out laughing, and the homophobic ones made fun of me, but the point was made, and it felt liberating to express. Ahmad took the courage and returned the sentiment, and then slowly, the rest echoed the same.

Was a deep moment. We were all kids living away from home, trying to find a path forward in life. I knew my road to enlightenment was basketball. Ahmad felt the same way, too. We became brothers for life, and started rolling together any- and everywhere to feed the hunger.

Ahmad jumped on my wagon of not missing a day without playing ball no matter what, to the point where we'd both be exhausted a lot of the time. My lil' bro could fall asleep anywhere and at any time. We used to joke around that he had narcolepsy. Maybe he actually did. The morning after the 76ers won the 1983 NBA Finals, there was an air of unforgettable, almost palpable excitement in the hallways at Lower Merion. Every student was celebrating the W, even the wrestlers and lacrosse players. Ahmad's health education teacher was none other than Coach Manning, who got upset with him when he nodded out during class. Manning ordered Ahmad to stand in the corner. Bro still clocked Zs, even when vertical on his two feet; not even the period buzzer woke his ass up.

When Ahmad and I got back to New York for the summer, I invited him to roll with me to watch the college division of the Pro-Am at the Borough of Manhattan Community College. We were the only two people in the stands during warm-ups. The tournament director walked over to us and explained that his scorekeeper and announcer hadn't shown up, and asked if we were interested in filling in. Uh . . . yeah!

Ahmad did the books while I excitedly grabbed the mic. I'd never announced a game before, but I used all the fantasy that the "Amazing Gumbs" had created at King Towers as reference. "Welcome! We have a capacity crowd of 5,336 today . . ." was my opening line. The place was completely empty. On an early play, a guard dribbled down the left side of the court with his right hand. I got on the mic, "Oh no, somebody forgot to bring their left arm!" A couple of players on the bench started laughing. I had an audience, so that egged me on, but the tall man running the show came right up on me quick fast and instructed, "Just say the score and personal fouls, kid." I might've listened, but homeboy didn't have any other options—plus, who walked in fashionably late at halftime? Future College Player of the Year Walter Berry aka "The Truth." Walt

Courtesy St. John's U. Athletics

proceeded to drop forty in the second half, and I couldn't contain myself: "You can't guard him! He can't be stopped!" I was certainly being biased and unfair to the losing squad, but who cared? Ahmad and I didn't get invited back to repeat our duties, but I was golden. My first time on the PA couldn't have been any more fun.

I walked out of the gym that night more enthused to play college ball than I had ever been. I set out to play in as many summer tournaments as I could again, and still keep my regimen of practicing, doing drills, and playing pickup. I started hitting a few more parks I had heard about that had decent pickup. Sunday mornings at 77th and Riverside had a rep, with Rucker legend Carlton "Moto" Greene as a regular holding court. I pulled up and had to rub my eyes to make sure I wasn't seeing a mirage, but lo and behold, both Pat Cummings, the 6'9" NBA center, and Thurl Bailey, the 6'11" anchor of 1983 NCAA champions NC State, were mixing it up in the paint. It was rare to see players that tall in the park, much less two of them in the same game. I wasn't able to get in on a next before they broke out, but it was cool to see them ball. Inspiration was unavoidable in the city.

Goat Park was still ground zero, and that summer I happily reconnected with my old Holy Name teammate Alix Achille, who was prepping to play varsity at La Salle. This older man with a little potbelly kept coming to watch us. He eventually introduced himself as Fashion Institute of Technology assistant coach Bear, and invited us to scrimmage with their squad down on 27th Street. I honestly wasn't sure if dude was being honest at first, as he didn't hand us a business card, didn't look like a former ballplayer, and didn't wear any FIT team gear. Nonetheless, Alix and I took him up on his offer. We arrived and immediately met the head coach and some players, so that was a relief. We ran a few fulls, and there was one kid who had the super-bungees. On one break, I pump-faked the defender left, then lobbed the ball up high on the right, and BANG. Homeboy cuffed it with two hands. I'd never thrown an alley-oop before. I felt like I had dunked the ball myself.

Coach Bear walked us out and shared that FIT's student body was "roughly 80 percent women, 10 percent gay, and 10 percent straight men," and that we should consider playing there. Until this pitch, it hadn't dawned on me that we were being recruited. Even though I wasn't interested in a two-year school and was decisive about not being back in New York for college, I still had to pinch myself. I'd worked three years toward one goal, and although the opportunity wasn't the right move, it had come knocking on my door. Fittingly at the Goat.

I returned to Lower Merion with momentum for my senior year in the fall of 1983. The ABC House had a host-parent

program where each of us would be placed with a family one Sunday a month during the school year, and I was matched with pop star Patti LaBelle and her husband Armstead Edwards. What?! Ms. Patti would sing in the kitchen as she'd prepare dishes I'd never heard of like vegetable tempura. At the ABC House, Charlotte Hunter became our new resident tutor. She had taken a year off from Wesleyan University in Connecticut, and I really hit it off with her. I was already up on the school because my Westgate neighbor Lincoln Parker was studying there as well. Considering Wesleyan was one of the top-rated small liberal arts colleges in the country, and the universe was planting people in my path from there, it became my first choice and I applied. I thought I had a strong chance of getting admitted.

And since I had made the honor roll, our ABC-LM guardians Milton and Diane relieved me from mandatory study hall daily from seven to ten p.m., which meant I could play under the lights at the Ardmore Avenue court any night of the week. My life was improving.

Our squad at Lower Merion was predicted to win the Central League and we were ranked in the preseason top fifteen for Southeastern Pennsylvania, led by Eric Jones, a 6'2" slasher who topped all CL scorers his junior year and was a legit D1 prospect. We also had 6'5" sharpshooter Peter Barton, who was bound to attract scouts to our games. Since they were our first two options and both roamed the perimeter, we ran a motion offense as opposed to the traditional dump-it-down-low-to-the-big-man-and-clear-out style, which was great for me because the paint was never clogged. The downside was that as the fourth option of the starting five, I wasn't always lucky enough to have the ball swung to the left side of the court where I roamed. Our point guard Tim Shaw was right-handed, and always started the play going right. That meant for me to get the rock, there had to first be three or four passes. When E and Pete were hot, that just wasn't happening.

Ultimately, I wanted to be a team player and contribute to us winning, so not seeing the ball as much as I would've liked was secondary. I understood my role. Starting in the fall of 1980, I'd had a goal of playing high school varsity and I was living it to the fullest. I did have my moments of frustration, though. Early in the season, we were in a holiday tournament that included nationally ranked Camden featuring Kevin Walls, who had just dropped eighty points in a game (and wound up averaging an uncanny forty-six ppg that season), as well as local powerhouse Martin Luther King Jr. HS, who we went up against in the first round. We were getting waxed in the first half. They had us on lock. Eric and Pete weren't in their rhythm, so on two possessions, I tried to take charge and brought the ball up, then shot before MLK could even set up their D. In this day and age, a "shoot first" point guard is completely acceptable, but in '83–'84 it was like I had performed sacrilege to the position. "Robert, what the hell are you doing?" Coach Manning ripped at me during halftime. "You gotta pass the ball!" I was so accustomed to turning the other cheek anytime someone was aggressive with me physically or verbally, and I'd never talked back to an authoritative figure, but I'd hit a turning point. "That's not fair, Coach!" I shouted at his same volume, which shocked him and everyone else in the locker room. "Why don't you say that to Eric and Pete? They shoot whenever they want, and you never say anything to them."

We got blown out that game, and the bus ride back to Ardmore was deafening silence. I didn't know if I was going to be thrown off the team or wind up in the doghouse the rest of the season, but I was glad I had stood up for myself. The thing was, I could back up my claim. Statistically, I was shooting 55 percent from the field, while Eric and Pete were both at 50. I felt I had every right to get as many shots as they did. I was a 5'10", 155-pound shooting guard, though, with no interest from any college programs, so I got it: I was going against the system.

To Coach Manning's credit, the next day in practice he huddled us all up. "We have a new rule, starting today," he announced. "There will be five passes on every possession before anyone shoots—no exceptions—and you will get benched if you deviate . . ." My respect for him tripled that day. Coach didn't directly say he was wrong, but his action spoke volumes either way.

ead, and he ... une final period to keep them on top. Senior guard Rob Garcia helped out with 13 points and some fine ball-handling. Duane Young had 18 points for trath Haven

We won eight of the next nine games with this new strategy and finished the season as the Central League champions. Along the way, Coach finally called my number for some plays that wound up being buzzer-beaters or game-winning shots. As my confidence grew, I oozed out a little more of my New York style in bits. In a blowout against Strath Haven, a defender jumped with me and was about to block my shot, so I spun in the air to avoid him and wound up making my first 360 layup. I had never even practiced one; it just happened.

One day in practice, Coach Manning had a booger in his nose, man. Every player on the squad was looking at it, but no one stepped up and said anything. So I told him. Coach wiped it off, and then he instructed us to run suicides under twenty-eight seconds as he always did. In my head, I responded, *Yes, Boogie Nose,* but I didn't dare say that out loud. I caught the giggles, though, and for the rest of our workout, every time he spoke to us, I kept hearing in my brain, *Yes, Boogie Nose, yes!* My shoulders were shaking from trying to stop laughing. I didn't want to be disrespectful. I honestly loved the man. Coach shouted out, "What's so damn funny, Robert?" and I literally almost blurted, *Nothing, Boogie Nose, nothing at all,* but I still just said it in my mind. Oh boy. "Back on the end line—you're all running suicides!"

The next game, against Marple Newton, Coach benched me the first three quarters as a consequence of my imagination. I was tight! I put that energy toward playing hard in the final period, though, and wound up with eleven points and seven rebounds in eight minutes. I wish I could've played like that all the time. Especially versus Springfield, against whom I had hit the back-breaker to win the game the first time we met, but in the second match, I was purposely fouled with six seconds left on the clock and had a chance to put us up by one if I hit both shots from the foul line. Their coach called a wise time-out to make me sit with the pressure. As I walked to our bench, one of the Springfield players passed me way too close and said, "You f*cking wop . . ." I had never heard that term before, so I asked Coach Manning what it meant in the huddle. He explained, "It's a derogatory word for Italians." I responded, "But I'm not even Italian, Coach!" "Don't worry about that, Robert. Just make your shots." I missed the front end of the one-and-one, and we lost.

### 1983 - 1984 STATISTICS

| | Field Goals Made | Field Goals Att. | Field Goal Pct. | Free Throws Made | Free Throws Att. | Free Points Pct. | Total Points | Point Av. Per Game |
|---|---|---|---|---|---|---|---|---|
| Eric Jones | 151 | 302 | 50% | 55 | 77 | 71% | 331 | 15.8 |
| Peter Barton | 176 | 353 | 50% | 101 | 122 | 82% | 442 | 16.4 |
| Jack Cuskey | 121 | 257 | 47% | 56 | 74 | 76% | 299 | 11.5 |
| Mike Simms | 93 | 167 | 56% | 33 | 62 | 53% | 219 | 9.5 |
| Tim Shaw | 13 | 29 | 45% | 8 | 20 | 40% | 32 | 2.0 |
| Mark Tabor | 21 | 60 | 35% | 21 | 28 | 75% | 65 | 3.6 |
| Robert Garcia | 58 | 106 | 55% | 15 | 34 | 44% | 131 | 6.2 |
| Dan Katz | 6 | 9 | 67% | 1 | 2 | 50% | 13 | – |
| Mark Brogan | 1 | 6 | 17% | 0 | 2 | – | 2 | – |
| Don Curtis | 9 | 28 | 32% | 3 | 14 | 21% | 21 | – |

While getting dressed in the locker room, I started crying. I was disappointed in myself and felt like I had let down our squad. I'd shot 55 percent from the field on the season, but a dismal 44 percent from the charity stripe. I knew I could do better. Being called a slur, whether correct or not, also gave me grief. Why would an opponent try to be so hurtful? Over a game? Was it really worth it? What was wrong with sports? What was wrong with our society?

We were matched against North Penn in the first round of the districts, and days before the game I twisted my ankle like a wet rag. The trainer was taping me up in the locker room when Coach Manning came to check my mobility. "I don't think you should play, Robert," he said with conviction. My foot looked like it had swallowed a softball. I stared him dead in his eye, and with all my sincerity said, "Please, Coach. Please . . . I have to." I didn't want to deal with the disappointment of a DNP for such an important game.

Manning gave me the green light. I got on the floor and dealt with the pain but couldn't really contribute how I would've liked to. My effort was valiant, though. We lost, which was an anticlimactic way to finish the season after the high of winning the Central League title. Lessons learned, though, and I could live with myself knowing I'd tried my best. I kept repeating the saying, *It's not whether you win or lose, it's how you play the game.* That became my mantra.

My high school playing career was over, but as one door closed, another opened right back up. That spring, I received a letter of acceptance to Wesleyan University. And unrelated, shortly after that I finally lost my virginity. I'd had enough with the Catholic guilt, but I was also realizing that I was such a product of my environment, being Puerto Rican where Christianity is widespread and growing up on 97th Street just steps away from Holy Name Church. What if I'd been raised somewhere else? Who would I have become? Living in Pennsylvania for two years really broadened my horizons. I started seeing the world with a new lens and did a lot of self-reflection. The moment I had opened up to the possibility of having sex for the first time, an opportunity presented itself. I had zero idea of what to do once my classmate had me in her bedroom, though. I sheepishly asked her, "Are you ready for the gold?" Jeeeeez. I was such a cornball! As soon as "the act" was over, I literally thought in my head, *Why does everyone rave so much about this? I could've been playing ball right now.* I was a rare bird indeed. Maybe a dodo bird?

The academic year finished, and I was elated for graduation, until my father showed up drunk to the ceremony. He'd done the same when I completed eighth grade at Holy Name as well. Was a little embarrassing, but I kept my head up. I could only be grateful to too many people for the whole experience of going away to school for two years. At this point I had only missed one day of playing ball in four years, and that was because I'd run a fever. I was also the only player on our Lower Merion squad who had 100 percent attendance coaching at the Ardmore Optimist clinic for the two years I could be there. I was gonna miss the kids I taught there, my teammates, my ABC House crew, Patti LaBelle's family who took

# Lower Merion wins in OT, takes Central League title

2/18/84

Robert Garcia hit a jumper with 25 seconds left to give the Aces a 39-38 lead and a free throw by Jack Cush...

me in so warmly, and all the other people in the Lower Merion HS and Ardmore communities who had shown me dookey love.

At the same time, I was amped to get back to New York for the summer. Maybe *too* amped. After graduation, I wanted to ponder everything going on in my head, so I passed on the car rides offered and walked by myself from the campus back to the ABC House. To do so, I had to walk over the train tracks at the Ardmore station. I'd done this route hundreds of times in the two years I lived there. Sh*t, I used to walk from one station to the next via the dark-ass tunnel to avoid the cops after hopping the turnstile back uptown, so daytime and outdoors felt light. This time, though, I was too deep in thought. The sound of an approaching Amtrak does not travel far ahead of itself. There's a little bit of delay. I didn't pick up on the metal trembling. When the conductor hit the horn twice, I turned to my left, froze, and then stepped backward off the gravel. One second. Two seconds. Three seconds. *Whoosh* . . .

Eight cars passed me going a hundred miles per hour. I felt the breeze. I could've been a wrap. That was my first real brush with death, but as soon as I got back to New York, I had another. Darryl Roberts and I went to Central Baptist to put up some jumpers, and on the way back to the crib, we heard a *pop!* The Fourth of July was a week away, so I just thought it was firecrackers. Darryl calmly said, "Oh sh*t, duck . . ." and before we both bent down behind the car in front of us, I looked across the street to the southwest corner of 95th and Amsterdam. Another *pop*, and another. A dude had gotten shot in his chest three times, right in front of a telephone booth. The cat holding the gun took off toward Broadway. Time stood still, then two police cars with sirens screaming flew through red lights on the chase. Darryl and I waited a couple minutes, then we continued our path uptown. I was impressed at how well he kept his cool. In my head, I heard the older dudes at the Goat telling me, *If I had a chance to do it all over again . . .* I was like, *F dat, let me live my life to the fullest while I'm here.*

Tomorrow may not be guaranteed.

The Bronx
aka the Boogie-Down BX
where the beat
met a rhyme
went all-city
then took over the world
This is the borough that
does not exist on an island
but ball handlers will leave you on one
on the way to the Baja
The Bronx keeps creating it
Highways can't divide
ballplayers from finding the sun
This is where a tiny man
with a ball in his hand

can munch on the truth
and become a master
The home of champions
where people who play ball
cannot be defeated
even if they take an L
No take-backs
the BX goes straight up
Somos jugadores callejeros
tenemos que jugar duro
Get a bucket and one
cross your arms
and put an X sign up
The world recognizes
the Bronx is everywhere

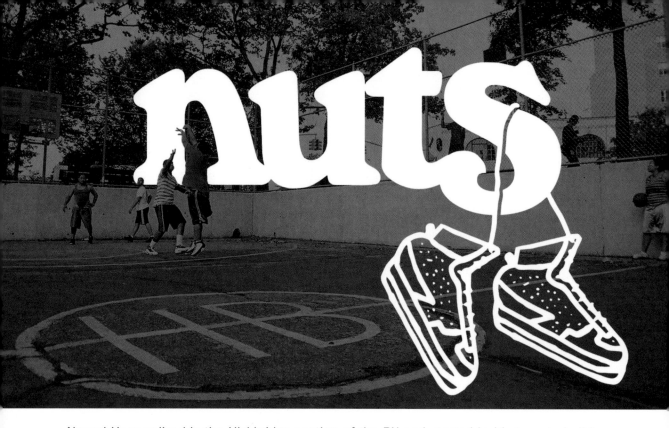

Ahmad Hooper lived in the Highbridge section of the BX and started inviting me to ball in his hood. It was a bit of a trek walking from the 4 train on 167th to the ridiculously steep staircase up to his block. Felt like the air was gonna be thinner that high above sea level. I'd help old ladies carry their shopping carts with groceries. Was a great workout. Worth the sweat, too, cuz we'd get to play 21 at Nelson Park against "Master" Rob Hockett, who one game left us both on our donut. Rob had the freak handle and knew how to kiss the backboard from the wing like it was his soulmate. He went on to become a legend in the EBC Tournament at Rucker Park throughout the late eighties and nineties, plus play for the Harlem Globetrotters, deservedly. His game had juju.

Nelson Park was also the home to the Flo Jo Classic, which was completely epic for me to witness. The concrete stadium seating would be packed. Ahmad and I would sit on the top row. On one play, "Cornbread" caught a breakaway. The court wasn't long, and when he got to the foul line, I noticed 1984 Juco Player of the Year Walter Berry at half-court sprinting to get back on D. I don't know how, but when Bread went in for the lay, Walt flew from the dotted and rubbed his shot on the boards. The announcer simultaneously yelled out, *"Brrr, stick'em, ha ha ha, stick'em!"* on the mic, which was the popular opening line to the Disco 3's hit "Human Beat Box." To add insult to injury, "The Truth" then cuffed the ball in the air on his forearm before coming back to earth. Before he could dribble, the spill-out happened. Cats were running in every direction screaming in joy, "Oooh! Oooh!" Pure euphoria. I'd only seen this happen at the final seconds of championships, but this was a regular-season contest—and only the first half. Pure New York. The game stopped for several minutes until heads settled down again.

At halftime, an unsigned beatboxer named Emanon performed on the mic. The Disco 3 (who by then had changed their name to the Fat Boys) and Harlem's Doug E. Fresh had really put the art form on the map, though I had never seen anyone make music with their mouth live. That whole park was transfixed by his talent, as was I, but the magic show was far from over. In the second half, Lamont "Tip Dog" Thornton led a two-on-one break, stopped at the foul line, and dribbled the ball high while simultaneously motioning his arms as if he was going to pass. His hands extended past the rock while never touching it, though, which blocked the view to the defender, who sprinted to deflect the dish that never happened. The place exploded. With no one in front of him, Tip got the bucket easily. Meanwhile, his opponent never stopped running, and hurtled past the crowd at half-court, then exited through the fence and continued down Woodycrest Avenue, never to be seen in Highbridge again.

You know how when you're a kid, and you see a martial arts flick, then you come out the theater trying to drop-kick your best friend, like, "Hiyah!" That's how I felt at Nelson Park. I was already hungry for b-ball, but witnessing Walter Berry, Emanon, and Lamont Thornton be so ridiculously creative and imaginative made me *thirstball* to do the same. Ahmad put me down on his Highbridge Gardens Community Center three-on-three squad. This was the first time I'd ever played in a half-court tournament, and with only two teammates instead of four, I was bound to get a ton of touches. I blossomed in that context. Ahmad's peoples kept asking him, "Yo, who dat whiteboy you keep bringin' around?" Ahmad would reply, "He not white, yo. He Puerto Rican." And then they would offer, "Whatever he is, he got a nice game . . ."

We didn't win much, but it was the first time I was really having fun playing under the whistle cuz we had no coach to scream at us, and rarely had a sub. That meant I didn't have to worry about getting benched if I tried a fancy pass and my teammate caused a turnover cuz they bumbled it. There were some bum teams that I got bizzy on, but there were also some great players, like Chuck Martin aka "Chuck Wheat," who later became a star guard at St. Raymond's HS and got inducted into their Hall of Fame. There was a buzz about how nice the fifteen-year-old already playing in the seniors division was going to become. I was like, "Chuck Wheat is nasty with it *right now.*"

The ooh-la-la factor of that neighborhood though was John Morton. When we played against the incoming senior all-city PG out of Walton HS, heads came out thick to watch, and I found out why the hard way. Morton's teammate shot a long jumper, and I happened to be under the rim innocently waiting for the rebound. Yet no one boxed John out, so as I jumped for the ball, his nuts literally bumped the back of my neck, and then he caught a one-hand tap dunk on my head, BONG! I'd never been dunked on.

BONG!

Photo courtesy of Seton Hall Athletics

Was not a great feeling, especially in front of a crowd.

In 1989, John Morton led Seton Hall to the NCAA final and dropped a game-high thirty-five points in a one-point loss to Michigan, then played in the NBA. While I was happy for him along that run, I can't front—every time I'd see him on TV, I'd relive getting yakked on by him. At the same time, watching him was a source of pride, because we were both named all-tourney at the end of that Highbridge Gardens three-on-three season. I didn't dominate any of the strongest players there, but I earned respect from them, which was a confidence builder.

All roads led back to the Goat, where "Dr. Ray" Echols and I went at each other all summer. The St. Raymond's HS guard had all the confidence in the world since his squad was top-ranked in the city. I couldn't guard him, and didn't have a fifth of the self-assurance he had, but . . . he couldn't stop me, either. I had never really felt like that until the summer of 1984 after playing in Highbridge. Ray and I wound up getting cool. "Dime con quién tú andas, y te diré quién tú eres . . ."

Ray's teammate at St. Raymond's was Norris McAdoo aka "Lunky Mac," and he would bring the sharpshooter to the Goat to run with us. Lunky didn't have a full right arm, so could only dribble, shoot, and pass with his left hand. Ray and I always knew exactly which way he was going to drive, and still couldn't stop him. Lunk was limb-different and got buckets. He didn't focus on what he *didn't* have. My mentality shifted. I declared: "So what I can't dunk. So what I'm not the tallest, strongest, or fastest. Whatever! I can still love this game more than anyone I know." Wooord.

I arrived at Wesleyan University in Middletown, Connecticut, in September 1984 fueled by my playground vitality, and with one goal in mind—make varsity. I played on campus daily without fail. Local legend Roger Younger was a D2 first team all-American at Sacred Heart U., and his little brother Albert was projected to be the town's next star. I befriended him while playing at the "small gym." Some evenings I'd ride my Raleigh ten-speed into town

to search for pickup by the housing projects. Albert noticed and told me I was the first dude from Wesleyan he'd ever seen in the hood looking to play. He also mentioned he appreciated that I didn't treat him like a "townie," a term some of my elitist classmates would use to describe people from the community. I didn't think nothing of it. That was my MO everywhere I went.

College life provided a lot of flexibility, but I was not managing priorities well. I wound up on academic probation. I was going to class, I just wasn't studying and doing assignments in between. Luckily, I was still eligible to try out for the team, but only made JV. My ego felt punctured. I also felt isolated. I was only one of seven Latinos in the entire freshman class of almost seven hundred students. One evening during Sunday snacks at the dorm, a hallmate went on and on about how much he hated the Puerto Rican Day Parade. I let him expose his scathing words because I was curious as to how ignorant he was. Eventually I interrupted him with, "You know I'm Puerto Rican, right?" He backpedaled and started profusely apologizing. I just shrugged the whole conversation off.

Toward the end of my second semester, my grades slipped even more, and I wound up on *strict* academic probation. Not only was I in jeopardy of not being eligible to play my sophomore year, I was also headed to getting kicked out of the school, period.

I had to ask myself, *Do you want to live a life of regret? Or do you want to try your best in this situation to move forward?* My parents had no clue about my grades. Turning things around would have to come from my own determination. So I did. Eligibility maintained, I then applied the same positive thinking toward making varsity finally, but once again I was put on JV. I was clearly not in the plans, and that was a tough pill to swallow. I was barely getting by in school, and was getting no play on the ball squad or from women. My esteem

was sinking faster than my body in a pool (and I still didn't know how to swim).

Leroy Darby kept me afloat that second year at Wes. The freshman from the Bronx was exuberant, brash, and *very* hip hop. One night after practice he walked down the steps at the dining hall spinning in a circle with his arms acting like propellers while singing the Beatles's "Here Comes the Sun" for no good reason while six hundred students watched him. He just didn't give a f, and I loved him for that.

Lee felt like a playful younger brother, especially when his pops would ship a care package chock-full of chocolate chip cookies. We'd gobble up a whole bag in one sitting.

Rakim's line, *"No tricks in '86, it's time to build,"* described the summer between my sophomore and junior years. I bumped into my former trainee Mike Parker on the old block. Mike had gotten a tad preppy in private school plus a little cocky from his success on the court. He looked me up and down, then threw a dart: "Yo, Bobby—what's up with your gear, man?" I had jokes and could snap, but I had no comeback as he had thrown me off guard. "All you wear is tournament shirts every day. Step your game up, b!" Mike had good intention, but he played me like an out-of-tune ukulele. He did have a point. My wardrobe was hand-me-downs and b-ball unis. I had never gone shopping for anything else, except . . .

Kicks.

I balled every day. I needed sneakers that performed and could last on the asphalt. Function aside, mystique and style also mattered—greatly. The blue chips were getting the dookey limited-edition releases. I wanted to look like them, but not for vanity. Anytime I had on an exclusive color, I'd catch opponents, least in New York, staring at my feet. Sometimes that helped me get picked up for a next; other times I gained a mental advantage over a defender. If my uni matched my kicks, that was gravy sauce for my confidence on the court, too.

I wanted my feet to be totally original. I'd put a box on ice for five years before breaking out the pair inside, or I'd customize uppers with leather spray in flavors no one, including the brands, had ever imagined to freak yet. I was expressing my individuality, but only below my ankles, or when I had a ball in my hand.

I only had three front teeth, so my budget dentist suggested I try braces to shift them, yet he wound up filling my new gap with a fake tooth that did *not* match the color of my real joints. My boy Ted "Nitro" snapped, "It looks like a nugget, Bob, a Chicken McNugget, stuck in yo' mouth!" I took the jokes and kept smiling regardless. I needed a new look, though. I contemplated getting my nose pierced, which at the time was unheard of for any dude I knew.

My teammate Mike Arcieri took notice of my burgeoning transformation, and pointed out that Wesleyan's coach was an old-school, conservative white man, who could frown on my lifestyle choices. I told Mike that how I presented shouldn't have any effect on me making varsity and getting minutes. He agreed, but shared that was only in theory. The reality was I had gotten cut two years in a row, so I owed it to myself to not give coach any more reason to do so again. "Play by the rules, Bobby," my mentor offered. I responded, "I'm not a conformist, though," then revealed that I planned to pierce my nose. "Whatever you do, please do not show up to school with a stud on your face . . ."

So I pierced my ear instead.

\* \* \*

I arrived at Wesleyan for my junior year rejuvenated, with a new look and attitude. I danced in class, boogied at parties, turned into a social butterfly at Olin Library, and quickly became popular on campus. I was still first and foremost a ballplayer. No way was I losing my identity as one. I was expanding my personality, though, becoming multidimensional in character. People started calling me "Bobby Nice," partially because of my game, but mostly due to the fact I just didn't stop smiling all the time. It was infectious.

At preseason workouts, I made sure I was once again the first to arrive and last to leave. I feared I couldn't run a mile under six minutes, but I clocked in at 5:50, which was my best time ever. Tryouts had me nervous, too. I had absolutely nothing to lose, though. I thought I played well during the scrimmages. There were four returning senior guards, and three underclassmen at the same position who had suited up varsity from JV the year prior. Of those seven players, six were white. Did the coach have a racial bias? There were Black players on campus who certainly believed so. If true, I had no idea how me being a Latino of mixed race factored in his head. Whichever way, my chances were slim. I still had my hopes of making it regardless.

On the second day, I barely felt a part of what was going on. Players were being cliquish, huddling up and joking around. I was the outsider. If this was my last day with a college practice jersey on, then so be it. I tried to comfort myself with the conviction that not one person in that field house loved basketball as much as I did. Wasn't a knock on any of my friends on the squad, more so a way to frame an impending doom with a positive outlook.

The following morning, the list of who made varsity went up on the corkboard with a thumbtack by the main entrance. I went way early before classes so I could be by myself. I still believed I had a chance to fulfill my dream of playing college ball. I looked for my name on the paper. I double-checked. My eyes got watery. I was nowhere to be found. Cut, a third year in a row. I stared at the eight-by-ten sheet, hoping somehow it was wrong. It wasn't. I grabbed my pen out my book bag, and on the top of the page, I wrote, *Where's Bobby Nice?*

I walked out of the field house in tears.

"I THINK
YOU'RE
READY"

Getting cut from varsity might have been the best thing for me at that stage of my b-ball career. I lost a lot of time for personal growth my freshman and sophomore years sitting on the bench, traveling to away games, and standing around in practice learning plays that were not fun for me to run. I'd feel like a robot. There was no creativity encouraged. My eyes lit up when JV opponents threw a full-court press at us. I'd go into "Pac Man" mode and beat the pressure off the dribble. I was used to breaking double teams from playing 21 all my life. This was also my way of signaling to anyone in the gym that yes, I may not be on varsity, but you looking at a brother who got game. Maybe my penchant to flex handle was why I didn't make the squad three years in a row. Either way, I wanted to turn a negative into a positive, and committed to becoming a better player than I ever was before. I had a lot of free time to do nothing but.

Steve and Larry Usher were twins from Mount Vernon who had an intramural squad called the Right Mix, and as soon as they found out I wasn't on varsity, they invited me to join. I wound up averaging twenty-five points that season, and we lost in the chip. I welcomed the camaraderie, which helped me avoid the winter doldrums of my sophomore year. A bonus of getting cool with Larry in particular was that he had a car. Nell's on 14th Street had just opened up, and we would drive two hours back home on the slim chance that we'd get into the hottest club in the world. We'd stand for forty-five minutes while freezing, two underaged twenty-year-olds trying to look cool, until *boom*—the velvet rope would open, and we'd be signaled in. There was an unrecognizable world on the other side of that exclusive entrance. Supermodel Jill Goodacre and I danced

together one night, until she asked me to wipe something off her glasses. I was like, "What I look like? Do that sh*t yourself!" Otherwise, that spot was legendary gold. DJs Frankie Inglese, Jules, and Basil would hold it down behind the decks, but my favorite selector there was Belinda. I'd never heard a woman spin, and she brought a different vibe to the dance floor. Larry and I would shut that spot down. I never wanted the party to end. The music and scene was that euphoric.

Driving back to the city more often allowed me to stay connected with my old teammate Ted "Nitro," who stayed up on all the latest street slang. Ted was the first person I ever heard use "hype" and "dope" to describe something that we would say was "fly," "fresh," or "def" in the early eighties. The Harlemite was also a sharp sneaker connoisseur. When Nike reissued the Air Force 1 in the winter of '86–'87, Jew Man's in the Bronx was the only store in all of New York that had them, and very few people were up on it. Ted caught wind, and called me up

at Wesleyan with divine words: "Yo Bob, what size are you? I gotchu, b!" My brother took the risk of getting vicked, then shipped me a white/blue pair. The model had gone out of production in '84, so receiving what had been my favorite pair of kicks to ball in ever was like giving the mighty Thor his hammer. It was on! Ted kept me two steps ahead of the game, literally.

Getting into Nell's and owning Air Force 1s were both extremely exclusive, and I took neither for granted one bit. I wasn't getting everything in life I hoped for. I still wanted to play college ball. It had been denied me. I still played every single day. I didn't know any other way.

During spring break, I found myself at the Goat one sunny day, no joke, on fire. I was not missing. "Cookie Puss" Tim asked me how my season went. I told him, "Nah, b—I got cut." "You? I guess your coach don't like Soul Food!" There's no way Tim could have known how meaningful it was to hear that. Being back around the way was healing. Ray Diaz, who played pro in Puerto Rico and was still a terror to guard, came up to me afterward and said, "Bobby, I think you're ready."

"Ready for what?"

"Puerto Rico . . ."

The hairs on my forearms stood up like a drill sergeant had screamed, *Attention!* The Arecibo Capitanes of PR's Baloncesto Superior Nacional (BSN) were courting Ray, but he had decided to pursue another career. He recommended to the owner, Dr. Hiram Ruiz, that I take his place. No effin' way this was happening. Was too good to be true.

Based on the strength of Ray's word, the franchise signed me to a contract without ever having seen me play. I finished out classes for the semester, and by mid-May I was on a flight to La Isla del Encanto. While waiting at baggage claim for my luggage, a huge 6'8" dude walked up to me and said, "Bobby García?"

I replied, "Yep, that's me."

"Bienvenido a Puerto Rico . . ."

On the car ride from San Juan to Arecibo, I asked, "How did you know who I was?"

Ismael Rosario, the starting center, offered, "You're wearing Air Force 1s. Only a ballplayer would have those on." I thanked Ted in my head.

At my first practice, empowered by the confidence Ray Diaz instilled in me, I went off. Our coach, Chago Maldonado, didn't speak a lick of English. My Spanish was limited to palabras básicas como *jugo*, *leche*, etc., so I couldn't learn any of the plays off the bat. That initially worked in my favor. My only choice was to revert to natural instincts. Studder step. Behind-the-back. Penetrate. 360 behind-my-neck pass. Pull up from fifteen on the break. Glass work. Bong bong!

The following day, the owner told me, "I heard you put on a show last night!" I was in heaven. My hotel room was two minutes from the ocean and a forty-minute walk to a secluded beach. I could go to the crib of the team's cook for three free meals a day. The manager blessed me with Converse Star Tech high-tops, unis, warm-ups, etc. I had access to the gym—*whenever I wanted to shoot around*. The kicker was—I was getting paid on top of all this? I would've easily played for free. Easily.

Our first contest was an away game at Bayamón on May 24, 1987. Ruben Rodriguez from PR's national team dropped thirty-one on us, and I was in awe watching from the bench. We got blown out, and Chago put me in during garbage time. On my very first possession, I pulled from the top of the key on a fast break off the dribble, and *kapow bang!* I was in the books. The buzzer sounded, and then another *kapow bang* from the stands. Someone got shot as people ducked under the benches or ran toward the exits. It was then that I noticed the court was surrounded by a fence as a protective measure for the players. *Bienvenido a Puerto Rico,* is all I heard in my head.

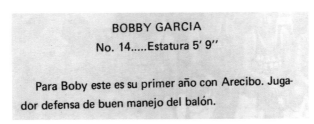

**BOBBY GARCIA**
No. 14.....Estatura 5' 9"

**Para Boby este es su primer año con Arecibo. Juga-dor defensa de buen manejo del balón.**

The team's program guide came out, and the caption under my photo said, *Jugador defensa de buen manejo de balón.* I couldn't believe it. Whoever wrote that recognized I had a handle. I thought I'd been penalized at Wesleyan for having one, but in a pro context I was getting props for it. Being in Puerto Rico was boosting my confidence every day I spent there. At the same time, it was helping heal the wound of getting cut from varsity.

Coach Chago decided to switch around our lineup, and told me I was going to start for the first time against the 1986 BSN champions Los Polluelos de Aibonito on May 27.

My father showed up for the game drunk, just as he had for my graduations. During the pregame huddle, Dad kept repeating my name to get my attention: "Robert García! Robert García!" I got that he was ridiculously proud, but it really threw me off. I was embarrassed. I still didn't know any of the plays, and this wasn't a scrimmage at practice or garbage time at the end of a blowout. I was expected to run the team.

My first shot attempt got punched, which led to a fast break the other way. The arena got loud. Aibonito's fans played congas, maracas, the clave, and guiro in the stands. Chago was screaming at me from the sideline, and I couldn't hear him, much less understand what he was saying because of the language barrier. I was being guarded by Willie Meléndez, a BSN leader in career assists. None of my teammates were moving or cutting to the basket, and since I was a little taller than Willie, I decided to pull from behind the three-point line. He jumped with me, though, so I double-pumped to avoid getting blocked again—twenty-five feet away from the basket. Was not a smart move. The ball missed the rim by two feet and thumped the backboard. Chago's hands went on his head in frustration as I sprinted back on D. Everything played in slow motion until the buzzer went off. "Sub!"

I'd had a chance to turn my season around, but blew it.

After the game, my father stumbled in the stands, just as he had in front of Alicia's Market when I was working as a delivery boy. I went over to help him as he looked up at me, slurring his words to say, "Robert García! Robert García!" He was so proud of me. I was fulfilling his own dream of playing pro on the island. Losing games as well as a chance at starting again were a lot smaller issues than the bigger picture at hand. I was a part of something that both of us had worked years for. That empowered me.

Our next game, on May 31, was against Los Leones de Ponce, led by Butch Lee, who was a bad, bad man. Lee had been the MVP of the 1974 PSAL champions Clinton HS, then received the same honor for Marquette in the 1977 NCAA final. The Harlem product who honed his skills playing pickup at Rucker Park then won an NBA ring as a member of the LA Lakers in 1980, becoming the first Latino to ever suit up in the league. He was also the starting PG for the national team when they lost by just one point to Team USA in the 1976 Olympics. In Puerto Rico, Butch was beyond royalty. His squad smacked us, and Chago put me in during garbage time. I ripped their guard at half-court, then raced down the other end for an uncontested two. I heard an old woman scream at me from the crowd when I scored. After the buzzer, I asked my father what she said. "¡Te cagaste encima!" my father shared. I looked at him, puzzled. "She said, 'You sh*t on yourself!'" Even though we were down by thirty, there was still no mercy from the fans.

That steal must've restored Chago's faith in me a little sumthin'. Our next game was against Fajardo with the BSN's leading scorer and MVP Georgie Torres, who wound up smashing nearly every career point record in league history. "Pretty Boy" was from the BX, and had all the bop bop from the playground. On a three-on-one fast break, Georgie jumped in the air, looked left, then wrapped the ball around his left-side rib cage so that it whipped back to the trailer on the right. My teammate was lost in the sauce. Even though I was on defense, I was like, *Wooord!* In my head, of course, not out loud.

In the last minute of this tight game, Chago subbed me back in, to my surprise. We were up two with twenty seconds left. Fajardo came down and passed the ball around the perimeter until I deflected it. I chased after the loosey, took two dribbles up-court, then whipped the rock to a teammate so I wouldn't get fouled and stop the clock. Buzzer sounded. We won! That didn't happen often in Arecibo that season, so our gym got festive like we'd just won the NCAA final. The owner came into our locker room afterward and gleefully offered, "Free hamburgers for everyone!" I sarcastically thought, *Wow, did he really just offer us burgers, yo?* I was done with fast food at that point because of a wack experience with a woman who worked at the local Wendy's. She was feeling me but spoke no English, and I couldn't swing *nada* in Spanish, so we would just smile at each other. She nicknamed me "Platoon" because I had a crew cut like characters in the popular movie by the same name. Was cute. One night, she asked my roommate about hanging with me after she got off, and instead of homeboy hooking me up, he tried kicking it to her himself. The nerve!

I romanticized playing pro ball, and the whole experience was surreal, but there were downsides. The cutie from Wendy's aside, I had no social life in Arecibo outside of the team. And most of my teammates were grown-ass men with apartments, some with kids, so making time to hang with me was an afterthought. The most exciting thing to do at night was order an egg sandwich from the food truck, pray they wouldn't put mayo-ketchup on it, and watch the viejos play dominoes in the plazita. I spent a ton of time by myself, walking to the rocks by the ocean to zone out to the sound of the waves crashing.

Solitude aside, I was having the time of my life. The practice before our game against Guayama, Chago asked me to play like their star point guard James "True" Carter, a crafty ball handler out of Baisley projects in Queens who had the in-and-out-dribble magical status and penetrated to the Baja whenever he wanted. Coach wanted me to prep our starting five by basically going nut. If only every coach could have turned me loose like that.

Toward the end of the season, I guarded Angelo Cruz, a fan favorite on the national team who played for Los Indios de Canóvanas. "Monch" was also a playground legend out of Patterson projects in the Bronx who talked mad smack. I scored twice and he told me, "Motherf*cker, you ain't sh*t." Then he sized me up and continued, "I'll bust yo' ass!" I was like, "Chill, b, it ain't that serious!" He was trying to intimidate me. Was all in the game. Well, at least I thought it was. I gladly never found out.

I played that rookie season on the worst squad in the league. We finished 6–24. I didn't get much playing time, and my stats were not impressive. The pride I gained in my heart by competing in my homeland was immeasurable, though. I had many identity issues growing up as a Boricua who couldn't speak Spanish. Black opponents in Harlem would call me *whiteboy*. Two Puerto Rock stickup kids in my hood once did the same. On my visits to the island as a kid, even my cousins would call me *gringo* when I couldn't understand what they were saying. By suiting up for Arecibo, though, I visited fourteen cities during our away games and saw with my own

eyes how ridiculously gorgeous the biodiversity was, from the mountains to the shores, the palm trees, the bioluminescent bay, the rainforest, the coquis singing at night, the roosters crowing in the morning, and all else the enchanted tropical country could offer. I saw the farmlands my mother was raised on in Barrenquitas. I played on some of the very same courts my father balled on in Rio Piedras thirty-five years prior. For the first time in my life, I felt a spiritual connection to my heritage, one that no one could ever detract from again moving forward.

Aside from a boost to my self-identity, the other major takeaway from that season was my improved self-esteem. When we played against Carolina, the game was televised on WAPA-TV. Chago signaled for me to sub in, and I'm not gonna front—I was type nervous. I'd never played on a live broadcast before. As I ran up the sideline, my teammate Gilbert Miranda, who barely got any playing time, grabbed my hand and pulled me toward him. Gilbert looked me dead in the eye and said, "Confianza." I didn't need a translation.

That simple gesture might've been the most effective support I received from anyone in the entire franchise the month and a half I was there. I felt seen, and that came from a dude I was taking minutes from who did not have to express compassion. The moment was empowering, and a reinforcement of the person I wanted to continue to evolve into.

Wesleyan and Yale played the very first intercollegiate contest in basketball history back in 1896. To my knowledge, I was only the second pro ballplayer my school had ever produced in the ninety-one years of its program. And . . . I hadn't even played varsity. Something felt really off with that equation. I had never heard of a senior making the squad after getting cut three years in a row prior, but I decided I would not be deprived of my dream. I set a goal to try out again. No fear of failure. F dat. What D3 coach in their right mind would not want a player with experience against Olympic athletes in a league considered top five most competitive in the world?

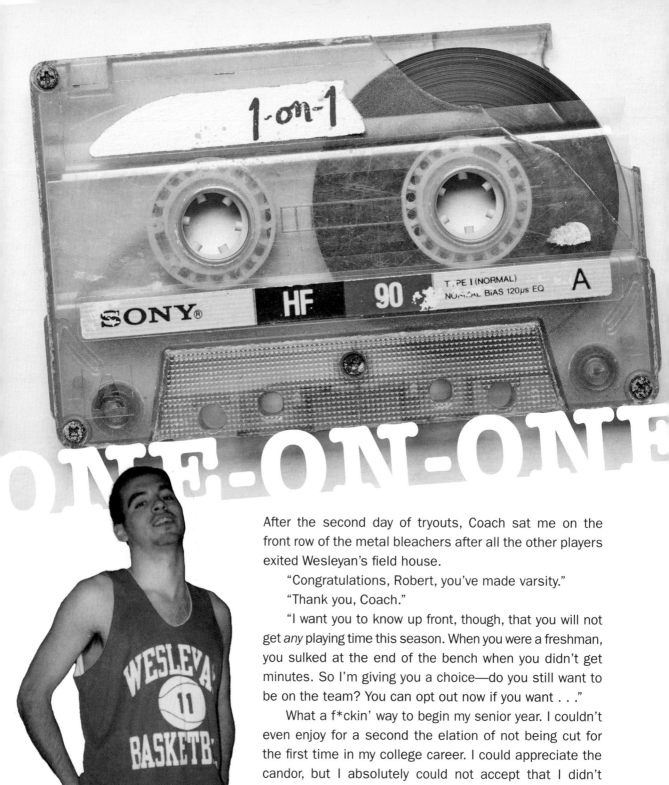

**1-on-1**

SONY HF 90 T·PE I (NORMAL) NORMAL BiAS 120μs EQ A

ONE-ON-ONE

After the second day of tryouts, Coach sat me on the front row of the metal bleachers after all the other players exited Wesleyan's field house.

"Congratulations, Robert, you've made varsity."

"Thank you, Coach."

"I want you to know up front, though, that you will not get *any* playing time this season. When you were a freshman, you sulked at the end of the bench when you didn't get minutes. So I'm giving you a choice—do you still want to be on the team? You can opt out now if you want . . ."

What a f*ckin' way to begin my senior year. I couldn't even enjoy for a second the elation of not being cut for the first time in my college career. I could appreciate the candor, but I absolutely could not accept that I didn't deserve playing time, or that I couldn't earn it by going hard in practice, especially with our new assistant coach Tom Labella around. The mastermind behind Middletown HS's record seventy-six-game win streak and three consecutive state championships from '76–'78 took an immediate liking to my game. During tryouts, I did an in-and-out dribble to a crossover, and I heard him go, "Ooh!" After I scored, he told me, "Nice move," in a really encouraging way. Hearing that from a staff member was completely foreign to me. Maybe with Labella on board, I had a chance to earn minutes.

"I want to be a part of the team . . ."

I truly wanted to say I played college ball. I had only missed three days of playing since 1980 when I decided that was a goal of mine. I'd spent seven years working toward it.

In our first few games, Coach kept his word and did not give me any playing time. I thought about my Arecibo teammate Gilbert who cheered me on even though he was firmly planted at the end of the bench. I used his example as inspiration, and followed suit. I wasn't going to sulk this go-round. I willingly stepped into the situation with complete knowledge of where I stood. I had love for the players on the squad anyhow, especially Leroy, who was stomping on our competition, so there was a lot to get amped about.

On December 3, 1987, we were in a tight battle with Merchant Marine. Up by two with twenty-nine ticks to go, we called a time-out. As my teammates went to sit on the bench, I encouraged them on by saying, "We got this, fellas," while giving out high fives. Then I cheered, "C'mon, let's GO!"

Coach shouted, "Shut up!" and the next thing I knew, his clenched fist landed right on my chest. He was crouched down in the huddle on one knee with his back to me. I hadn't seen that coming, and didn't know how to react. No one on the team did, not even Labella. We all stood there . . . stunned. I wasn't aware at the time that I could have reported him to the athletic director for misconduct. I had fourteen witnesses.

The next day at the beginning of practice, Coach huddled everyone up and shared, "I want to apologize for my actions last night . . ." He didn't mention me, or make eye contact my way, just made a broad statement to the team that was flat and meaningless. Leroy and I glanced at each other, and he shook his head. After practice, Lee said, "He just does not like you."

I replied, "Nah, b, I think it's something deeper than that." I wasn't trying to figure out that puzzle, though. I simply wanted to play ball. Wasn't there for the politics.

The upside of the season was that our squad was nice. We came close to a #1 ranking for New England D3 schools in February, and only took one L at home leading into an ECAC playoff berth. The field house would get packed, and when we'd blow out our opponents, a section would start chanting, "We want Bobby Nice!" I'd get in during garbage time and would crowd-please with a fancy pass or move. In my best performance, I scored on four successive possessions and tallied nine points—in sixty seconds. Didn't count for anything, but I had the bleachers going nuts every time I touched the ball.

I was hesitant, yet I invited my father to the last home game of the season, Senior Night. He hadn't visited me on campus the whole four years I was at Wesleyan. I didn't want a repeat of that embarrassing moment in Aibonito, or a reenactment of the 1987 movie *Hoosiers* when actor Dennis Hopper portrays an alcoholic parent who shows up drunk to his son's game then draws a costly technical foul

**WESU Sports Present:**

## Men's Basketball vs. Amherst
## 7:50 Saturday

THIS IS IT. One of the most important and long-awaited sports events in recent memory is coming to Wesleyan- and WESU SPORTS is there! The Amherst Lord Jeffs- highly touted and ranked #1 among all Division III Northeastern schools try and stop the red hot Cardinals. The showdown will have an enormous impact on the playoff picture, as well as the Little Three Championship. If you can't make it to the gym, your walkman or radio will allow you to catch every exhilarating moment. Steve Almond, Len Besthoff and Andrew Siff bring you all the action live from Alumni Hall starting at 7:50. Don't miss history in the making.

*WESU SPORTS 88.1 FM*
*- THE BEST IN COLLEGE SPORTS RADIO*

from the ref for arguing about a call on the court. When I saw that scene in the theater, I started bawling. That sh*t felt too real. I knew all too well the roller-coaster ride of hoping a family member could manage one of their vices, only to deal with the disappointment and repercussions when they didn't.

The last home game had a lot of excitement leading up to it. Senior cocaptain Rob James was sure to reach one thousand career points in the first half. We were also going up against our Little Three rival Amherst, who was ranked #1 among D3 New England schools. Lastly, we had a six-game winning streak that gave us momentum for our most important match of the season.

Senior Night fell on February 13, 1988. The field house was packed like I'd never seen it. I was on the layup line during pregame warm-ups. I looked to the sideline, and my father was there taking photos . . . sober. My inspiration to pick up a basketball in the first place just nodded at me with a graceful face expressing without words, *I'm here, don't worry. Do you.*

Dad hadn't seen me play ball like that since . . . I beat him one-on-one the summer of '81. My heart started dancing. I caught extra adrenaline and started grabbing the rim, doing three-hand claps, reverses, dips (now called jelly), etc. I could've earned Layup Line All-American that evening (if there was such a thing). The buzzer sounded, and all players returned to the bench for the announcement of the starting lineup. Finally, my time to shine . . .

**ONE-ON-ONE**

"And now, the starting lineup for your Wesleyan Cardinals tonight. Let's give a nice round of applause for Leroy Darby . . . Ed Googe . . . Pete Alberding . . ."

The crowd was juiced up, but I was completely confused . . .

"And let's give a nice round of applause for our senior cocaptains playing in their last home game, Brock Ganeles . . . and Robert James!"

What the f*ck, man? Senior Night was a decades-old tradition. I was supposed to go out on the floor, play for however many minutes, then get subbed out so the crowd could give me my due. Why wasn't I out there? Especially the first time my father had ever seen me play an organized game while he was sober. What was going on?

Robert James scored his 1,000th point, and the crowd threw toilet paper on the court. We beat Amherst 86–82 in one of the most celebrated Wesleyan victories in years.

I didn't get one second of playing time.

The next day at practice, I truly did not give two f*cks about anything. We scrimmaged, and I played possessed. I blocked a jumper, ripped my man dribbling, called no plays, and just went nut every time I touched the rock. I was not missing, and scored as if my honor depended on it. Afterward, I couldn't stop breathing heavily. I sat on the third row of the metal bleachers with my eyes balled up, and started wailing. Leroy ran over and hugged me. That was comforting, though I couldn't stop crying. I just let it all out.

The Wesleyan Argus, February 19, 1988                                    15

# CARD ⚜ GAMES

## Red-hot Cards rout Emerson by 72

### Wes' streak at eight; Williams battle looms large

By Andrew Siff

Our next game was on February 17 against Emerson. We were up by thirty-five at halftime, so coach subbed me in, and I played the second half. I scored ten points and had seven assists in nineteen minutes, and relentlessly attacked the rim. I wasn't trying to be classless to our opponents—I just had a lot of frustration to get off my chest, and the EC Lions just happened to be the recipients. My fellow teammate Brock told our school newspaper, "Bobby Nice *owned* the place." We won 125–53, setting two school records in the process: most points in a single game and largest margin of victory. Those two achievements have yet to be broken all these years later.

When our season ended, I was actually relieved. The bigger hurdle of graduating on time loomed ahead. Latinos in the eighties had the highest dropout rate and lowest college attainments of any US population group. I was one of seven in the class of '88. Only four of us were scheduled to finish in May. My senior essay was not approved, and days before graduation, I was doing successive all-nighters to revise my paper. With the amazing support of my academic supervisor, Professor Rob Rosenthal, I finally passed and was able to walk on time.

0098

**ONE-ON-ONE**

I finished in the bottom tenth percent of my class, but gave that no weight. I had beaten the odds by making varsity as a senior, and did the same by graduating in four years from one of the top five liberal arts colleges in the nation. Beyond anything I learned on the court or in the classroom, I strengthened my belief to not fear failure. Nothing was guaranteed. I could work as hard as possible, but there might be forces against me that were simply out of my control. So long as I gave my 110 percent effort, it didn't matter whether I reached my goal or not. I could live with myself and move on. That lesson had started when I was in high school playing at the Goat, which made me want to return home. I contemplated going back to Puerto Rico to play pro, but that was gonna take some uphill climbing on my part to make happen. After dealing with Wesleyan's abusive coach, I needed a break from organized ball anyhow.

I had no clue what New York had in store for me postgraduation, yet I vowed before leaving campus that twenty years later, Wesleyan's basketball program would know my name, somehow, someway. Meanwhile, the asphalt courts of the five boroughs were beckoning me. I needed to be part of a love-based community again, one where I would be accepted for being unique and where I could realize my full self . . .

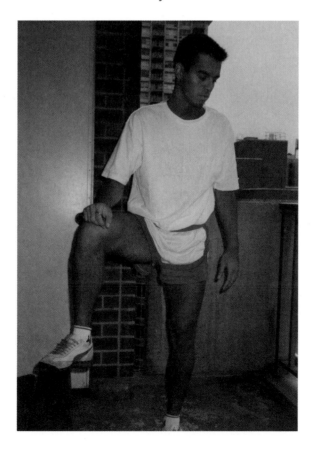

# LIVE AT THE BBQ

Being back in New York had a ton of benefits. Since I'd knocked out both goals of playing college and pro, I didn't really have a new destination to work toward. All effort moving forward was going to be based on experiencing the sport as lovely as I could. I no longer had to contend with a coach's mind games or malice. I didn't have to limit myself to the context of winning or even being in a game against opponents. In my heart, I was still in my early teens fascinated with the nuances of ballhandling, and in love with the style and culture that the playground fortified my soul with. I no longer had to compromise my creativity. In fact, the more inventive I became, the more attention I received.

There was a move I developed in the late eighties out of curiosity and a drive to be original. It started with a Pistol Pete Maravich stationary drill where he'd do a V dribble on the side of his body, back and forth while bouncing the ball as hard as he could. I thought, *What if I did the same motion, but in between my legs?* To achieve it smoothly, I needed to lift my foot for the catch behind my back in my "blind spot." Once I got that down, I imagined the scheme in forward motion. Took weeks of practice, but I'd fantasize that there was a defender running alongside me on the break who would bite for the fake once I dribbled rigorously between my legs while turning my head in the direction of my teammate trailing. When I caught the rock to go forward, the D would be lost, and I could slide to the hole uncontested. I needed to test this theory out.

The first time I unleashed the move was during a five-on-five at the Goat. I raced downcourt, and at the top of the key I defied conventional basketball with exuberance. The defender was dumbfounded as he kept saying, "What did he just do? *What did he just do*?!" Shortly after, I had a tournament game in Harlem at PS 194 on 144th. I had a two-on-one fast break with my teammate trailing, and BOOP! When I scored afterward the whole gym exploded. "That's Soul Man!" I heard two kids shouting in the stands while pointing at me. They were referring to Jimmy Tate, a celebrated Entertainers Basketball Classic (EBC) trickster who caught hood fame while playing at the legendary Rucker. Other than our skin tone, Jimmy and I looked nothing alike. I still took the reference as a compliment. I was being likened to a ball handler who had a rep in the world's most famous outdoor arena. That became aspirational.

I'd never seen anyone attempt what I had invented, not even close. I pushed the envelope, and that just cracked open my brain to explore more. I started wondering why I'd even wasted my time playing college ball. Don't get me wrong, had I had a different experience I would have never thought that. I did realize that organized sports were not for everyone. And that was okay. For me, uptown was where the life of the party was, where I felt most comfortable, and where I wanted to stay. I didn't mind jumping downtown to go clubbing, though.

One night at Nell's, I bumped into my old teammate Mark Pearson, who introduced me to two up-and-coming MCs named Pete Nice and MC Serch, as well as Dante Ross, who was doing A&R at Tommy Boy Records and had signed Queen Latifah. Pete and I hit it off immediately as he was an all-Brooklyn/Queens selection for Bishop Ford HS. Mark told him I had some game, too, so the respect was from jump. As the party hit its peak, Serch and I made our own circle and danced our asses off. From that point on, we all became unofficial crew.

Me and Dante Ross at Car Wash

Mark and Pete wound up becoming roommates, and one night Dante came over to play the unmastered, unreleased cassette of De La Soul's debut album. We all sat there transfixed. No one said diddly-squat. We just bopped our heads and listened in astonishment. That was the moment when I realized I wanted to work in the music industry. Dante was my inspiration and blueprint. He'd started out as a messenger for Rush Artist Management and paid his dues up the ladder. I hoped for the same opportunity.

w/ Cey Adams @ Def Jam Office '89

Lo and behold, Pete and Serch got signed to Def Jam Records, and they helped plug me in for a jay-oh-bee as a messenger starting in April of 1989. My gamble to not chase playing pro a second season in Puerto Rico and instead stay in NYC to explore mos def paid off. I couldn't care less that I had a prestigious college degree while making five bucks an hour. I had my foot in the door at the world's number one rap label. Just like Dante, I got promoted with the quickness and wound up running college radio/club/mixtape promotions.

A lot of music industry cats as well as artists were hard-body b-ball fans. I was still sporting my tournament shirts and shorts as casual wear, and since I steady customized my kicks in colors no one else had, it was undeniable that the game was the pulse of my life. One of the higher-ups at Def Jam noticed, then tried talking sh*t to me, challenging me to a one-on-one. We went to NYU's Coles Center, and I literally spanked him 11–zip. Left him on his donut. He never again questioned whether I could play.

My favorite hip-hop-meets-b-ball moment of the early nineties was when Def Jam flew me to the BRE Convention in New Orleans. The biggest names in rap were on the bill—Public Enemy, LL Cool J, Run-DMC, Big Daddy Kane, and . . . Rakim. The next day, I went searching for pickup and landed at a local Y. The gym was so hot that they had fans the size of airplane propellers blowing in each corner. The "God" walked in with his crew, then we picked sides and ran a full. The tone was "nobody's smiling," just like his "In the Ghetto" song lyric. I went to the Baja and pulled off the same signature V-dribble fake to the trailer I'd first debuted at the Goat and then PS 194. Bong bong! Two of Ra's teammates snapped their necks in the wrong direction and I scored.

After the five-on-five, he gave me a pound while saying, "You got a nice game, g," and yo, I kid you not—Rakim let out a smile. I never even knew he had teeth. I returned the compliment then asked him if he had played in school before he became the world's most influential lyrical architect. "Football was my sport . . ." he shared. "But, you know, I played a little ball, too. Everybody did."

When the *Source* magazine moved to New York from their humble beginnings on Harvard's campus, their offices were a block away from our Def Jam headquarters on Broadway. Cofounder Dave Mays and editors Matty C and Chris Wilder all played ball, so I'd invite them to a run my boy "Chilly E" had at the Theological Seminary, which we nicknamed the "House of Pain" because invariably someone got injured there every time we played.

In 1990, the *Source* was revered as the bible for any hip hop head, featuring mainly album reviews, artist interviews, and regional reports. Cofounder and editor Jon Shecter wanted to expand the editorial to include culture and fashion, so he asked me to pen an article about kicks. My rep in the music industry—particularly among his staff—as a ballplayer with exclusive customizations was what made him believe I could pull it off. I'll never forget what he said to me when he offered the assignment: "You're *that* guy who should write it." I titled the piece "Confessions of a Sneaker Addict," and it appeared in the May 1991 issue. Unknowingly, I'd invented "sneaker journalism" in the process, as it was the first exploration of the cultural phenomenon in media history.

All of a sudden, the entire hip hop world recognized me as a ballplayer, as I had written the article completely from that perspective. Of all the T-shirts I could've worn for the photo shoot, I chose my Big Apple Games one to pay homage to the tournament that had helped inspire me almost a decade prior. I met dudes from North Carolina to Paris who told me they taped my article to their wall because it was the first time they had ever read something

that spoke volumes to how they felt. With "Confessions," I created a connection between basketball, hip hop, and sneaker culture in an unprecedented and authentic manner. I was grateful to the *Source* for giving my voice a platform.

In 1990, I met a young DJ at Def Jam looking for promo vinyl named Adrian Bartos. I hooked him up and we became tight immediately. Months later, the Columbia U. student invited me to start a hip hop radio program with him on the campus station, WKCR. From jump, our *Stretch and Bobbito* show made noise with listeners throughout the tristate area, some of whom played ball. During a game at Rodney Park in Williamsburg, I got fouled. When the ref handed me the rock to shoot, an opponent lined up and said, "That Redman freestyle y'all played last night was bananas, yo." I told him, "You're not gonna distract me from hitting this free throw, b, but we can talk about that after the game . . ." The smile dropped from his face as the rock said *dush* through the net.

In 1993, hip hop music video director Dave "Shadi" Perez was hired to do research for Wieden+Kennedy's global creative director, John Jay. The ad agency was preparing the launch of Nike's "City Attack" campaign. Shadi had read my "Confessions of a Sneaker Addict" article, and told John they had to get me on camera to talk about kicks. I tore that interview up! Shortly after, I got a call from the Swoosh's newly hired director of basketball marketing in New York: "Hi, this is Gerry Erasme, may I speak with Bobbito?"

The voice sounded too familiar. I replied, "Is this . . . Gerald . . . from the Goat?"

"Wait a minute, is this Bobby?!"

I hadn't seen Gerald since 1981, the summer when I completely fell in love with b-ball at the Goat and never looked back. He was one of my inspirations. How crazy was it that our paths would cross again? With him running point for Nike and John Jay making me

his "cultural DJ" at W+K, I was brought on board to consult on the "City Attack" campaign, doing everything from casting, location scouting, scriptwriting, product feedback, research, you name it. All the years I had spent nerding out about anything and everything related to NYC playground basketball culture became totally worth the effort.

As the brand's worth grew in the Big Apple, so did mine to their marketing strategy.

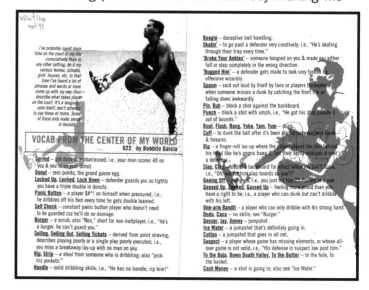

VOCAB FROM THE CENTER OF MY WORLD
022 by Bobbito Garcia

*I've probably spent more time on the court in my life cumulatively than in any other setting, be it my various homes, schools, girls' houses, etc. In that time I've heard a lot of phrases and words or have come up with my own that describe what takes place on the court. It's a language unto itself; don't attempt to say these at home. Some of these only make sense in bounds...*

**Served** – got done or embarrassed; i.e., your man scores 40 on you & you're on your donut.
**Donut** – zero points, the grand goose egg.
**Locked Up, Locked, Lock Down** – defender guards you so tightly you have a triple double in donuts.
**Panic Button** – a player $#*! on himself when pressured; i.e., he dribbles off his foot every time he gets double teamed.
**Self Check** – constant panic button player who doesn't need to be guarded coz he'll do no damage.
**Burger** – a scrub; also "Non," short for non-ballplayer; i.e., "He's a burger; he can't guard you."
**Selling, Selling Out, Selling Tickets** – derived from point shaving; describes playing poorly or a single play poorly executed; i.e., you miss a breakaway lay-up with no man on you.
**Rip, Strip** – a steal from someone who is dribbling; also "pick his pockets."
**Handle** – solid dribbling skills; i.e., "He has no handle, rip him!"

**Boogie** – deceptive ball handling.
**Skatin'** – to go past a defender very creatively; i.e., "He's skating through their trap every time."
**'Broke Your Ankles'** – someone boogied on you & made you either fall or step completely in the wrong direction.
**'Bugged Him'** – a defender gets made to look very foolish by offensive wizardry.
**Spasm** – said out loud by itself by fans or players themselves when someone misses a dunk by catching the front rim or falling down awkwardly.
**Pin, Rub** – block a shot against the backboard.
**Punch** – block a shot with umph; i.e., "He got his shot punched out of bounds."
**Bout, Flush, Bang, Yoke, Yam, Yum** – dunk.
**Cuff** – to dunk the ball after it's been placed between your hand & forearm.
**Dig** – a finger-roll lay-up where the player places the ball behind his head like he's gonna bang it, but then softly releases it over a defender.
**Slap, Clap** – slap the backboard for effect when you can't dunk; i.e., "Oh you got him slap boards on you?!"
**Geeing Off** – going off; i.e., you just hit five shoulders in a row.
**Geesed Up, Zeeked, Gassed Up** – feeling more proud than you have a right to be; i.e., a player who can dunk but can't dribble with his left.
**One-arm Bandit** – a player who can only dribble with his strong hand.
**Dodo, Caca** – no skills; see "Burger."
**Geyser, Jay, Jimmy** – jumpshot.
**Ice Water** – a jumpshot that's definitely going in.
**Cotton** – a jumpshot that goes in all net.
**Suspect** – a player whose game has missing elements, or whose all-over game is not solid; i.e., "His defense is suspect low past him."
**To the Baja, Down Death Valley, To the Butter** – to the hole, to the basket.
**Cash Money** – a shot is going in; also see "Ice Water."

I was, in basketball terms, a unique triple threat for them. Just like I could pass, shoot, or dribble once I had the ball in my hand, I could talk about b-ball, kicks, and hip hop just the same when they handed me a mic. Gerry hired me to host the 1994 Nike three-on-three, their first ever basketball activation in the city. I hadn't announced a game since my 1983 debut at the Pro-Am, but my tongue was sharp from being on the radio with Stretch, so I jumped right in. I crushed that so hard, they put me in the studio to do voice-overs. I wound up performing in forty TV and radio ads, one of which went national during the Knicks's playoff run against the Pacers.

Backtracking, I wouldn't have gotten Nike love had I not written the *Source* article. I wouldn't have gotten in with that publication, or Stretch on the radio for that matter, had I not worked for Def Jam. And I wouldn't have gotten a gig in the record industry had it not been for my Upward Fund teammate Mark Pearson putting me in the mix with his basketball peoples. I was enjoying entertainment and all the opportunities it was presenting to me, but I never lost sight of my roots. The bottom line was I was a ballplayer first. And throughout the nineties I kept my feet planted firmly on the asphalt no matter how much attention I was getting from hip hop, media, or multinational corporations.

Like Dean Meminger once said, "If you don't ball, you can't hang out." I wanted to hang out. I wanted to play ball more, though.

# GAME DAY

My favorite tournament to run in uptown during the nineties was the Ray Diaz Roundball Classic at the Sand Park on 100th Street. I looked up to Ray since he was the one who gave me my shot to play pro in Puerto Rico. Our squad was basically made up of all my best friends. One game, Mike "Boogie" Thornton (Tip Dog's brother) did something that I've never seen anyone else do. With his right hand, he simultaneously dribbled around his back *as well as* his defender's, catching the ball in stride back on his right hand—*all in one bounce*. My teammate vaporized as he hit a reverse dip, never turning around to see if he scored or not. He just ran back on D like, *Hi, it's a nice day.* That was some real Houdini sh*t.

Probably the most humiliating moment at Ray Diaz for me personally was when we got blown out by thirty to Tim Gittens's crew. He was still in high school at the time. On a fast break, Tim stopped at the foul line, smirked at me, then did a chest roll with the ball (a trick learned from his father who played with the Harlem Globetrotters). The ref called the game even though there were two minutes left. I was tight in the face. A decade later, Tim aka "Headache" became a star on the AND1 Mixtape Tour.

In 1995, Walker Wear founder/designer April Walker sponsored a team in the EBC at Rucker Park. They weren't winning at all, so with the season winding down, my homegirl asked me to come on board to see if I could help out. Man. The Rucker. That was as hallowed ground as one could get. Our squad was soon getting blown out by 6'8" guard "Alimoe" Evans, who announcers "Duke Tango" and Al "Cash" were egging on to get nice with the ball. Evans aka "The Black Widow" starting doing the spider drill—in game—as he dribbled forward before wrapping the ball around my teammate's back. Crowd was loving it. I was too. The energy was nuts.

When I subbed in, Duke showed me love by telling the crowd, "That's my man Bobbito from the Nike commercials!" That was welcoming as the crowd was otherwise not feeling our crew. I wasn't really feeling them, either, as they froze me out on offense and were petro to guard Alimoe on D. When I finally got the ball for the first time, I dribbled past the hash mark and then pulled from two feet behind the NBA three-point line as I usually would.

I didn't factor that I was shooting on the high rim at the park, though. The ball *barely* grazed metal. If the ref had taken a puff from one of the weed smokers in the front row, he might've called an air ball. Duke got on the mic and said, "Wait a minute . . . that's not Bobbito . . . that's . . . Danny DeVito!" Being compared to a 4'10" actor whose name rhymed with mine was mad hilarious. A thousand people in the stands thought so too, and let out a hearty guffaw in unison which was . . . *humiliating*. I couldn't front on the joke, though, and started laughing myself as I ran back on D.

I didn't score that game, and we got blown out by thirty, but I wouldn't trade that experience, or the tournament T-shirt, for nothing. I've met countless players around the world who would cut their right arm off to have had a chance to play at '55th aka Rucker Park in the nineties. Priceless.

The element of surprise was constant, no matter the borough. Former LIU guard "Buddah" invited me to run with him in Brooklyn's Tillary Park Pro Classic. We got blown by thirty-plus to a squad that featured 6'5" forward Obadiah Toppin (father to NBA player Obi Toppin Jr.). "Snoop" dropped forty on us, literally on eight threes and eight boofs. Do the math. He took no shots in between—it was either behind the line or *hong!* We weren't going to make a comeback, and the refs tried calling the game with three minutes left so they could go home early. We protested, and in the melee a kid snuck on the court, grabbed the game ball, and flung it over the fence. His homeboy was waiting to catch it on Tillary Street—in the middle of traffic—and then they both ran off laughing. It was a sh*tty rock, too. They just burped the tournament for giggles. That was comedy.

Being on squads that got blown out in multiple tournaments wasn't hard on me. I really held on to my teenage motto of, *It's not whether you win or lose, it's how you play the game.*

I had to guard Ty "Boogie" Davis in the East Orange Pro-Am in New Jersey one game. Davis was just coming off being the MVP of the 1993 D2 NCAA championship for Cal State Bakersfield, who finished 33–0. At Rucker, Duke and Al Cash nicknamed him Ty "Dangerous." His hezi could freeze a pizza oven. Ty looked at me like a vulture would a dead donkey. On the first play of the game, he told his teammates, "Iso!" He then scored on me—ten consecutive possessions. We only had five that game so there was no sub for me, and no-help D due to pro rules. That said, I played alright. I hit a few deep threes and made some nice passes, enough to earn Ty's respect after the final buzzer sounded.

Six years later, Ty was playing for Kingston in the Goat tournament, and we met in the chip. I knew better than to try to guard him, so I literally had six different teammates D him up throughout the match. Didn't matter: the 1999 Goat finals MVP lit my squad up for forty-two that night.

There was no shortage of amazing talent playing summer ball in NYC. Another game out in the East Orange Pro-Am, Stanford U. all-American Brevin Knight picked me up full-court. I did a half spin to a crossover that lost him, but . . . before I even got to the half-court line, the future 1998 NBA steals leader was right back in front of me. He was fast as sh*t!

In the Nickelodeon Tournament on 20th and First Avenue, I had the golden opportunity to play against 1984 NCAA champion Gene Smith of Georgetown. Gene was the backcourt anchor of the nation's top defensive team that season. I was nervous when he picked me up on D. After I made the first shot I took on him, I had to hold back from jumping for joy. *I scored on Gene Smith!* I'd seen him put the clamps on opponents and throw away the key. I went that whole game without getting ripped by him, which there's no statistic for, but it sure meant a lot to me.

Later that same season, Howie Hudson guarded me one game. This dude led all scorers at West 4th the same summer that Knicks forward Anthony Mason suited up at the Cage, as well as LIU star Charles Jones, the number one D1 scorer in the NCAA. I was intimidated, but reminded myself that I had played respectfully against Gene Smith. I went hard left on Howie, he bit, and then I *screech, halt!* stopped, crossed the ball to my right hand, and fled the crime scene. Howie lost his footing enough that his right hand touched the floor to stop from falling. Happened in front of the score table by the northeastern hash mark. I remember every detail of the moment because . . . that was the first time I ever cracked someone. I wanted to emulate "Pearl" Washington, who had a habit of making defenders fall with his in-and-outs, and I'd fantasized about it for years. I paid the price for skatin' on Howie, though. He scored fifty on us and led his team to victory. That man was no joke.

The experience of playing against top talent really helped me when I'd get down in more local joints like Asphalt Green, Ham Fish, and Dunk If You Dare on Avenue V in Brooklyn. One night, my brother Ray called me up last minute because his Lawyers League squad was short one player and he wanted to avoid a forfeit. I raced to IS 44's gym, and dropped a career-high thirty-five points.

01 11

Photos: Tamara Schlesinger

Months later, I was shooting around at Tompkins Square Park in the LES with this white dude dressed in khakis and Clarks, like he'd just got off work. These two herbs in freshly purchased NYU gear walked up and challenged us to a game of two-on-two. Khaki Pants could play. I threw him an alley, and he cocked it with two hands on both of the college kids, like, *Go find your mommy!*

My teammate's name was Adam Rapp, and he'd go on to become a Pulitzer Prize–nominated playwright and novelist. I immediately put him down in every tournament I had a team in, and he returned the love. That's how I wound up at Nickelodeon. Years later, he opened up about how we first met. I'd always thought it was at Tompkins Square, but he told me, "Nah, it was the Lawyers League." I didn't remember playing against him, though. "I had just finished playing D2 college ball. I moved to New York, and in my very first game here, you put thirty-five on me. Was quite the introduction to the city!"

My first taste of being on an upper-echelon squad in NYC was when Coach Sid Jones (rest in peace) asked me to run with his mighty United Brooklyn crew. The starting five featured three players who finished as the all-time leading scorers for their respective D1 programs: Buck Jenkins from Columbia, Ken Bantum of Cornell, and Boston U.'s Drederick "Ice" Irving (Kyrie Irving's father). I didn't get much burn, but the day Sid brought down Syracuse U. star Conrad McRae, we only had five, so he had to start me. Before tip-off, Rad aka "McNasty" told me, "When I'm in the post, look at which side of my waist I put my thumb on." I didn't know where the Washington Bullets's second-round draft pick was going with this. "If I point to the left, then just throw the ball in that direction. Doesn't matter how high, Bobbito. I'll catch it . . ." and then he winked at me. On our first possession, Rad's right thumb went up. He jabbed toward me, then cut to the basket. I lobbed the ball up high over his 6'10" defender in the post. BLAM all over his coco!

Would've been great to have an unstoppable force in the post like Conrad McRae as a teammate on the reg. That's something playground legend Ed "Booger" Smith certainly enjoyed when we played against each other at Masaryk Towers in the LES. The star subject of the documentary *Soul in the Hole* was a Brooklyn enigma who in 1997 *Sports Illustrated* called the "King of the Streets" in a cover feature article. I outscored him, but only because he kept diming "Hammer" in the paint after blowing past me whenever he wanted to. Hammer finished with fifty, and Booger easily had twenty assists that game. The Bed-Stuy magician could have put fifty on me, too. I was relieved that he enjoyed feeding his man more.

As recognizable as Booger was in the hood, there was one player in that same era who commanded even more of the ooh-la-la status. My boy Ted "Nitro" kept telling me about a HS kid at Rucker destroying the unlimited division named "Skip to My Lou" who everyone was talking about. Had tricky passes like Master Rob. Had a handle like Pac Man. Had the jellyroll finish like the extra-unstoppable Gerald Thomas aka "Dancing Doogie." I had a game one afternoon at Brookville Park in Queens. Our squad's captain added a skinny teenager to the roster for the day. I was relieved cuz I had already played in the East Orange Pro-Am earlier that afternoon, hadn't eaten, and was on E in the stomach tank. The kid threw the ball away a few times in the first half and looked out of his rhythm as I sat on our bench eating a hot dog. In the second half, though? I witnessed brilliance on the court as double teams were split, no-look dimes were passed out like a coin bank had broken open, and double-pumps in the lane were converted for buckets as if he was mopping the asphalt. After the buzzer I asked, "Bro, what's your name again?"

"Rafer . . ."

Rafer Alston would go on to revolutionize how basketball was played when footage of the genius exploded internationally via the AND1 Mixtape series starting in 1999. Alston would also go on to play in the NBA for multiple franchises, having a great season in '06–'07 where he finished top ten in the league for steals and three-pointers made. When I first saw him with my own eyes that afternoon in QB, I knew he was something special.

Rafer made it to the league, though not every legend out of the playgrounds was so fortunate. When I met Mark Pearson at the Upward Fund in 1982, he kept telling me story after story about his boy Jack Ryan at East 5th Park in Brooklyn. Jack averaged twenty-six ppg his senior year at John Jay HS, but pissed away multiple D1 scholarships with a don't-give-a-f attitude and poor grades. In his debut at West 4th, "Water" dropped forty-four points against Detroit Piston Phil Sellers and got named to the all-star game immediately off that sole performance. Hall of Famer Chris Mullin once described Jack as the best shooter he'd ever seen who hadn't played in the NBA. Sportswriter Peter Vecsey was a believer, too, and got the sharpshooter a tryout with the Nets in 1990. The twenty-nine-year-old was the second-to-last player cut.

Another product out of East 5th was "Turk" Gumusdere aka TRIKE1, Mark Pearson's graffiti partner who became the first Turkish-born D1 ballplayer when he suited up for Brooklyn College. Turk put me down on his Caton Park squad in Flatbush, which was a trek from uptown, but the crowd ate up my flashy play, so I told him I was down to run with him wherever. He took my word for it and included me on his Starrett City Pro-Am team in deep, deep Brooklyn. That meant almost two hours each way between the train then bus transfer, but I was a nutjob for b-ball, so I jumped at the opportunity. Halfway through the season, Jack Ryan walked in the gym. I had been hearing about his legend for almost a decade, so I trusted the folklore and fed him the ball. Jack hit his first seventeen shots, all from the

perimeter. We were down one with seconds to go, and our opponents were dumb enough to leave Water open in the corner. I penetrated and kicked it out to him. Instead of shooting, he pump-faked, drove to the lane . . . and missed the layup. Jack Ryan finished an incredible seventeen out of eighteen from the field, but we lost.

With the addition of Jack, our squad wound up winning the Starrett City chip easily. Jack dug playing with me cuz I set the table for him well, sacrificing my own shot attempts—but when you have a weapon who literally splashes 90 percent from the field, you gotta be out of your mind not to give him the rock as much as possible. Jack loved dribbling the ball behind his defender's back, through their legs, and straight embarrassing whoever guarded him, so suffice to say, we got along well. We had a game in the East 5th summer league against a squad filled with players who were firemen. On a fast break, I picked up the ball, whipped it around my waist a full 360 degrees while looking left, then passed to Jack who was cutting on the right. A defender, who busted through walls to fight fires for a living and was strong as an ox, jumped to block Jack's shot. Water took the body bump to draw the foul, then deliberately *tapped the rock* on the firefighter's forehead before finishing the layup in the air. The ref shouted, "And ooone!" That just added insult to injury. Their bench cleared. I thought we were gonna get stomped out like a window curtain in flames. Luckily, things calmed down, and we got out of there unscathed.

Jack and I in the backcourt together was straight *fun*. We wound up taking the chip at East 5th, too. Neither of us played much D, but Adam Rapp did, so we all entered a squad in the 14th Street Y Pro-Am where the comp was a few grades higher than East 5th or Starrett City. During the regular season, a guard named Jean Prioleau who played in the preseason with the Knicks straight dropped sixty on us. We also lost to Prime Time, a team stacked with former NBA and D1 players but were catalyzed by the omnipresent "Speedy" Williams, who had only played D3 at Medgar Evers. Whether I was on the mic announcing or playing against him, I watched him destroy in the Asphalt Green, Nike three-on-three

and Pro City, Almighty Force at Ajax Park in Queens, pickup at Roberto Clemente State Park in the BX, you name it. The star opposing player to Duane Martin at the Rucker in *Above the Rim* wasn't just a great scorer, defender, and leader. He was a sh*t talker who would trip you when the ref wasn't looking if it meant a W, too!

I did not like Speedy. Me, Jack, and Adam's crew had a chance to avenge our loss to his Prime Time team when we met them in the 14th Street Y final that season. We played the perfect game, sharing the rock, finding the open shooter, moving without the ball, and nailed an incredibly high percentage from the field as a unit. We couldn't stop the defending champs on defense, so we simply pushed the ball, hit threes on the break, and ran up the score in the hopes a track meet would land in our favor. And it did. I had never beaten a squad Speedy was on prior, and I've never won against him since, but for that one moment I got to taste what it felt like to beat the best. And that sh*t felt good! Craziest thing was that I earned two friends in the process. Jack and I became lifelong b-ball buddies, and Speedy wound up being a really cool-ass cat off the court. I guess I had to earn his respect first to see that side of him.

Aside from tearing my MCL in a pickup game in 1997, playground basketball in NYC during the nineties was an unexpected joyride. I closed out the decade in '99 on a high note by getting named to the Goat Tournament all-star game, an honor that meant the world to me because Earl Manigault had passed the year prior at the tender age of fifty-three. I always wanted to honor the inspirational legend. Playing on the courts named after him gave me solace.

Photo: Hugues Lawson-Body, 360 Creative

# "¡Donqu

"¡DONQUEOOOOO!"

# eooooo!"

The first AND1 Mixtape featuring Rafer Alston moved hundreds of thousands of units. That success prompted the brand to produce a follow-up. Waliyy Dixon aka "Main Event" hosted a game in Linden, NJ, that would be filmed for Volume 2. I was booked to DJ the event. While playing Mobb Deep's "Right Back at You," this dude with a ripped body asked me, "You Bobbito?" I nodded and gave him a pound. He held my hand and pulled me in for a long hug. "I was locked up for a while, b. You and Stretch's radio show held me down inside the belly of the beast. Thank you." I expressed gratitude in return to homeboy, particularly for being open enough to share. During my twelve years on air, I had a number of formerly incarcerated people tell me the same, and I felt empowered by each.

Before the game started, I left the turntables to shoot around since I had played with or against many of the players there, including Tim "Headache" Gittens, Shane "Dribble Machine" Woney, Malloy "The Future" Nesmith, and Anthony Heywood aka "Biz" aka "Half Man, Half Amazing." I had never met "I'll Be Right Back," but had been hearing about him at EBC. He did an inside hand change—behind his back. I'd never seen anyone do that before. The move was almost unimaginable because from the front view, the ball disappeared for a second. I couldn't believe my eyes. Headache shared that he used to watch me play when he was a shorty and had been inspired by my game, which pleasantly surprised me. Then he asked if I wanted to suit up. And like a big dummy, I was like, "Nah." I honestly was intimidated by the level of showmanship that I'll Be Right Back displayed. I should have played, though. Had I gotten one or two highlights, who knows . . . might I have been on the first AND1 Mixtape Tour? Not getting on the court is to this day the singular regret I have in my entire b-ball career.

As fate would have it, though, I would have another chance at the spotlight . . .

In 2001, I went to a tryout for the Nike "Freestyle" commercial at Boys Harbor.

The who's who of NYC tricksters were all there, including Larry Williams aka "Bone Collector," who would blow up at the Rucker months later. Harlem Globetrotter Arnold "A Train" Bernard stole the show doing tricks in a well-orchestrated routine. The Future also lit the gym up with his rhythmic dribbles and no-look passes. He moved as if he was dancing, which gave me an idea when it was my turn to audition. I started out with basic crossovers between the legs, then did one of my signature moves: a wraparound-my-waist half spin to

01 17

a drop where I sit on the ball and cross my arms in a b-boy stance. Crickets. I always got a laugh or "Ooh!" from the crowd in any park I ever pulled that off at, but the audience for this spot was the crème de la crème and no one was giving it up easily. So I picked the rock up . . . and danced. Doing "The James" was risky because the swivel-step slide was intricate, plus it was difficult to pull off with grippy sneakers. Cats burst out laughing, though, and that became my ticket to be on camera in one of the most celebrated basketball advertisements ever.

When I was a shorty, I dreamed of one day being a Harlem Globetrotter. Never happened, yet off my three seconds of fame in the "Freestyle" ad, I was gladly sucked into a world of entertainment basketball where—and I could have never anticipated this prior—I was getting paid to have a ball in my hand while traveling the world . . . doing tricks? Yes, doing tricks!

That road started with small shows alongside my 14th Street neighbor Ramón Rodríguez, who was nasty with the ballhandling, so I plugged him into the Swoosh's activities. Joined by the breakout star of "Freestyle" Luis "Trikz" Da Silva, the three of us did the Nike float at the Puerto Rican Day Parade, then performed in Taiwan with other cast members in front of thousands of b-ball addicts thirsty for the New York aesthetic. I had signed autographs for hip hop heads over the years, but that week in Asia was the first time I was responding to requests for my signature as a recognized ballplayer. That sh*t tripped me out.

And this was just the tip of the iceberg . . .

Jack Ryan, who was now being called "Blackjack," had been doing shows for the Harlem Wizards as well as solo ones as the "Hoop Wizard," so Ramón and I asked him to join us to form a group. We called ourselves Project Playground. A talent agency started booking us to do halftime shows. We eventually added other members, including Kenny Rodríguez, who later became a Harlem Globetrotter, and Jansy Gonzaléz, a dear friend but also the best freestyler in Puerto Rico at the time. Between the five of us, we performed for the Knicks at Madison Square Garden, the Hornets, the Mavs, the Spurs, as well as

NCAA national champions U. of Florida and UConn (men's and women's), plus countless other schools and camps. Every time the announcer would introduce us one by one over the arena's PA, I would be pinching myself. Like how unlikely was it that while I never made it to the NBA or played D1, I would still show their audiences how much I LOVED basketball in person?

While the recognition of me as a trickster was growing, my notoriety as a DJ was skyrocketing. In 1998, the *Source* magazine crowned me and Stretch with the title of "Best Hip Hop Radio Show of All Time." In 2001, I started a residency at APT, which quickly became the most respected club in the city for progressive music aficionados and dancers looking to hear rare Latin, soul, jazz, funk, rock, dance, breakbeats, Jamaican, Brazilian, and even ballads. Not one tune could be heard on commercial radio. I was curating an experience that was completely against the grain of what was happening in the downtown scene at the time. I saw it as being no different than approaching basketball and sneakers with a counterculture mentality. I simply wanted to feel inspired and unique, plus connect with similar-minded people who sought the same.

Me and my brother for life DJ Rich Medina at APT

The morning of September 11, 2001, I was trying to sleep in since I had spun at APT the night before, but my phone kept ringing. After about twenty missed calls, I reluctantly picked up, only to find out that there had been an attack on the World Trade Center. I was living on 14th Street at the time. I looked outside my front window, and there were hundreds of people frantic on the street. My block was the cutoff point. No one was being allowed to pass the police barricades to go farther downtown. The air was dense and smokey. I heard people crying on the sidewalk. The whole scene felt apocalyptic. So what did I do? What I did every day. I crossed the street and hit the Y. Not surprisingly, Ramón Rodríguez walked in, too. We both loved basketball like nobody's business, and had the gym completely to ourselves until LES legend Joe Skie joined us. Joe had been inside one of the Twin Towers when it got hit. Luckily he survived, and the first place he went to after that disaster was not his home, which spoke volumes about his passion for the game. The three of us shot jumpers together and tried to normalize an otherwise nutty day. I always felt like a court was my safe space. I never thought of it as a shelter, though. That day cemented my belief in its healing effects.

Photo: Kelvin Jones

One of my boys who passed away on 9/11 was Stephen Mulderry. We had been teammates at the 92nd St. Y Pro-Am. A few weeks before the attack, "Zip" was named the MVP at Ham Fish as his team won the chip. HF director Bill Lynch decided to dedicate the tournament in Steve's name for the 2002 season, and his team asked me to run with them in his place. That was big shoes to fill, but I accepted. I knew being a part of his circle would be healing for all of us. I played my heart out and we reached the finals, but lost in the end. No one was disappointed. We all paid our due respect to our fallen homeboy that summer. Bill awarded me the sportsmanship award for the player who most exemplified Stephen Mulderry's spirit. I was never one to care much about physical rewards, but that was the one trophy I most cherished receiving in all my years of balling.

My b-ball career expanded in 2003 when former *Vibe* magazine editor Jesse Washington and 1987 Indiana Pacer draftee Sean Couch approached me about partnering with them to launch *Bounce*, the world's first year-round publication dedicated to playground basketball. I had been writing freelance for *SLAM* since its early days, so it was a no-brainer to accept. My new partners then bugged me out when they asked if I would be on the cover of our first issue. I didn't feel worthy, so I asked, "Why me?" Jesse responded, "You epitomize the outdoor game and the signature NYC aesthetic." Sean added, "We want to leverage your popularity as a player and a music expert, too." I didn't know how to digest the praise. Then Jesse smiled and said, "Plus, we know you'll do something ill for the camera."

Photo: Ben Ortiz

That wasn't the only sportswriting I'd do that year. Dana Albarella launched Testify Books

Photo: Farel Bisotto, Sole DXB

and wanted me to write about kicks. She would go on to publish my debut title, *Where'd You Get Those? New York City's Sneaker Culture: 1960–1987*. I particularly documented how important playground basketball was to the burgeoning movement, how even hip hop took its cues from the ballplayers who roamed the courts with style. Between that project and *Bounce*, I was really able to flex my knowledge of the game. In both instances, I infused all my personal experiences and the history I'd read, plus injected the folklore I'd heard

"¡DONQUEOOOOO!"

from my friends and elders over the years. In essence, I added a new title to my growing list of capacities: b-ball historian.

I strived to represent the outdoor game as authentically as possible, so when EA Sports asked if I would be the announcer to their *NBA Street Vol. 2* video game for that very reason, I had to really think hard about whether I'd do it or not. I advocated for people worldwide playing ball on the asphalt, not virtually on their PlayStation or Xbox. I had no experience with electronic sports. The brand hired the Wieden+Kennedy agency's creative director Jimmy Smith to consult and produce. Jimmy was the rock star who'd put me in the "Freestyle" commercial as that was his brainchild, so knowing his pedigree, I decided to kick flavor on the mic.

I flew out to the EA Sports headquarters in Vancouver, and spent forty grueling hours over five days in the studio howling at the top of my lungs. The main gripe with *Vol. 1* was that the users who played endlessly would hear the same lines over and over. EA wanted the experience to be as unique as possible every time in *Vol. 2*. So, for example, they asked me to say "dunk" forty different ways. I told them there was legit maybe only ten variations on how to describe that move, but if they let me get loose, I could come up with some esoteric and completely nonsensical lines. The writers were all hockey players—not even kidding—and they were like, "Yeah, ad lib all you want, the more the merrier." So that's how I wound up recording, "That's like a pizza slice with no crust!" for a missed dunk. I also called up my boy Jansy Gonzaléz in Puerto Rico for some lines in Spanish that were popular en la cancha. That's how I added, "¡Lo dejó pegao!" for a defender who got crossed and fell, and my favorite, "¡Donqueooo!" ("dunk" en español).

I had nooo idea the impact *NBA Street Vol. 2* would have. From press to the grimiest block in the hood, it's been widely considered one of the greatest sports video games of all time, and many would claim the very best in the basketball category. In 2021, the Ringer produced a documentary about EA's iconic gem, and interviewee Marty Sliva earnestly said I was "maybe the best commentator in sports history." My voice was heard in millions of homes worldwide, over and over and over, for years. I was also an unlockable character that users could play with, which manufactured a greater view of my playing ability than I actually had in real life. People confused fantasy with reality, and some started calling me a "streetball legend."

Put the brakes on. Screech! Chill.

I detested the word "streetball" the same way that Crazy Legs felt about being called a "breakdancer" instead of a b-boy. In both instances, corporate America and the media pushed the incorrect terms to the masses. I've always felt our community should determine how we self-describe with our own language. I can't remember one instance in the sixties through the nineties where I heard someone in New York say "streetball." We referred to the sport as "playground basketball" or simply "ball." "You gonna play ball?" No one mistook that for baseball or football. We all knew what our fam was talking about. No other sport mattered to the devoted diehards of my city, myself included.

In the early 2000s, though, our style was getting packaged and sold. Brands and ad agencies had to quickly figure out how to market the lightning off the asphalt in a way that differentiated it from what HS, college, and the NBA were messaging. "Streetball" became *their* catchphrase for the movement.

The only place I've been to where "streetball" made literal sense was the Philippines. I

saw kids in Manila put up make-shift rims on the curb then play three-on-three in the middle of an intersection. They'd wait for cars to pass by, then get right into it. Otherwise, most action happens in the park, school-yard, playground, gym, sidewalk, fire escape, trash can, monkey bars, etc.

While the word "streetball" bothered me, being called "a legend" really made me feel un-

comfortable. I could accept that lofty status in hip hop and sneaker culture with confidence, but as a ballplayer? Corey "Homicide" Williams scored forty-plus on 2004 NBA Defensive Player of the Year Ron Artest (now known as Metta Sandiford-Artest) at Nike Pro City, then the next week put the same numbers on Smush Parker, the starting point guard for the LA Lakers from '05–'07. Corey dropped thirty—in the first half—at Dyckman, which caught the eye of the Toronto Raptors, who then invited him to free agent camp. The 6'3" menace was the last player cut before the final roster was made. When I played in Dyckman in '03, I went on my goose egg—for the entire season. Tournament director/announcer Kenny Stevens mockingly nicknamed me "The Writer." Corey was a play-ground legend; I was not. No way did I deserve to be

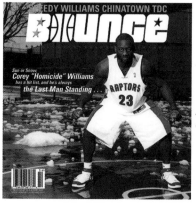

Bounce cover photo: Nicky Quamina-Woo

mentioned in the same sentence with him, or Joe Hammond, "Pee Wee" Kirkland, "Fly" Williams, on and on for that matter. I had too much respect for the game, and couldn't fake the funk. I would correct people when they'd acknowledge me as such.

I went from park to park, gym to gym, for twenty-plus years as a relatively unknown ballplayer outside of the small local tournaments/open runs I had gotten a little juice from. Things were never the same for me after my cameo in the Nike "Freestyle" commercial and voice-over work for *NBA Street Vol. 2*, though. Gone were the days of showing up at a court to play pickup and not a soul knowing who I was. And when I did get recognized, there was a target on my head for the first time in my life. Cats wanted to see if the hype was real. I now had to deal with expectations. I literally had no choice but to step my game up.

Photo: Chris DiNunzio

In May of 2004, I moved to Harlem, started jumping rope for conditioning, and went back to my early eighties MO of playing ball *every effin' day*. If I was gonna be at my best, I had to put myself in the most fertile b-ball environment known to mankind . . .

Harlem's claim to playing the best ball in the world may very well be true. During the Black Fives era (before the NBA was racially integrated in 1950), the most dominant team was the Rens, who called the Renaissance Ballroom on 137th and Seventh Avenue their home. They won the first ever World Professional Basketball Tournament in 1939, powered by Harlemites "Pop" Gates and John "Boy Wonder" Isaacs. In the '32–'33 season, the Black-owned franchise went a record eighty-eight consecutive games without a loss (not shabby considering the second-longest streak in US pro sports history is held by the Lakers with thirty-three). The squad, as well as individual members, have all been inducted into the Basketball Hall of Fame.

Harlem's Holcombe Rucker is the longest-running youth league in the world. Mr. Rucker invented the idea of organized outdoor summer ball in 1946 at 138th between Fifth and Lenox. Ruck would have kids run fulls, and kept the game clock on his watch, score on a sheet in his hand, and the schedule folded up in his back pocket. He even reffed, too. A true one-man show.

In the fifties and early sixties, his tourney grew considerably and added a college and pro division. Crowds on Seventh Avenue at the parks on 128th and 130th witnessed local legends like Ed Warner, the 1950 NIT Tournament MVP for City College who weeks later led his squad to a W in the NCAA final as well (the only school in history to win both

in the same season). Isaac Walthour aka "The Rab," who played briefly in the NBA for the Milwaukee Hawks, was uptown royalty and dominant. Westsiders coach Butch Purcell opined that Walthour was "a better ball handler and player than the wizard Bob Cousy." Cal Ramsey was the Rucker MVP one season. The original "Hawk" averaged twenty ppg and seventeen rebounds in his three years as an all-American at NYU. Another big draw from around the way was Tom "Satch" Sanders, who went on to win eight NBA championships with the Boston Celtics. Cars would be triple-parked while kids climbed the fence just to get a peek of the action.

Thanks to Holcombe Rucker, Harlem's faithful had the opportunity to watch the greatest players of the era—for free. Ruck laid down the blueprint for every organized outdoor summer basketball tournament, on any competition level, that has ever been produced since. He is the Godfather. The Granddaddy. Rucker also inspired generations moving forward to this day to want, or even better *dream*, of one day playing in New York, specifically Harlem, and particularly outside. He was the architect that transformed a simple, local asphalt court into being globally recognized as hallowed ground.

Unfortunately, Holcombe Rucker died of cancer in 1965. He was only thirty-eight years old.

In his years as an educator, coach, and community organizer, Rucker helped hundreds of Harlem youth get into better schools, using basketball as a tool. To commemorate his contributions, the city dedicated the park on 155th and Eighth Avenue in his name a few years after his passing. A committee formed to keep his youth league moving forward at multiple historic sites over the decades, including Harlem Lane, Dyckman, Mt. Morris (now known as Marcus Garvey Park), Colonel Young, Riverside Park on 101st Street, and Milbank, keeping the Rucker vision alive.

The Rucker Pro League, started in 1965 by Bob McCullough and Fred Crawford, was held at Mt. Morris before eventually moving to '55th aka Rucker Park. McCullough was mentored by Mr. Rucker in the fifties, and went on to become the second-leading scorer in the nation (right behind future Hall of Famer Rick Barry) with 36.4 ppg while at Benedict College. Codirector Fred Crawford also played for the Knicks and Lakers. With their connections, they had all the top NBA players of the sixties and seventies up in Harlem.

In 1971, Julius Erving finished his college season at UMass averaging 26.9 points and 19.5 rebounds a game, but no one in New York had ever seen him play, or even heard of him. That was, until his first appearance at the Rucker . . .

In the immortal words of my old United Brooklyn coach Sid Jones: "My friend told me, 'There's a Rucker player who is better than Connie Hawkins and Elgin Baylor, and can jump from the corner and dunk. They call him 'The Claw.'"

Erving told the announcer that his nickname was "The Doctor," and a playground legend, as big as there ever was or will be, was born. The NCAA didn't allow dunking in that era, so with the crowd *ooh*'ing to his above-the-rim assaults, Erving kept elevating his creativity to heights unseen in that era. "Dr. J" went on to win championships, MVPs, scoring titles, and dunk contests, in both the ABA and NBA, and is widely considered one of the most influential players ever. Essentially, he was the Michael Jordan of the seventies. Erving completely credited his summers spent at the Rucker as the catalyst to his style of play.

How tough was the Rucker Pro in 1971? The league MVP that season was "Tiny" Archibald, who in '72–'73 led the NBA in both scoring (34.0 ppg) and assists (11.4), a feat never accomplished before or since. One of Erving's teammates was Charlie Scott, who in '71–'72 led the ABA in scoring with 34.6 ppg, and eventually won an NBA chip in '76 with the Celtics. With all that firepower, Erving and Scott didn't even win the '71 championship at '55th.

While Erving, Scott, and Archibald all got plenty buckets in the NBA, Harlem legend Richard "Pee Wee" Kirkland finished as the top scorer at the Rucker that summer. A Chicago Bulls draftee who never played in the league, "Stickman" wreaked havoc on the best that ever played the game while talking *a lot* of smack. He once crossed up Charlie Scott so viciously, Scott's sneaker fell off.

While Kirkland was a dangerous scorer, his backcourt partner Joe Hammond was arguably *the* deadliest shooter in NYC history—ever. "Our Milbank teammates used to complain they weren't getting the ball," Pee Wee once said to me. "I'd tell them, 'Shoot the rebound if we so happen to miss!' People thought 50 percent was a great field goal percentage, but that meant they missed just as many shots as they made. Joe would hit 80 percent from the field on anyone, day in and day out. So I fed him . . ."

Nicknamed "The Destroyer," Hammond had a rep at the Rucker that earned him a tryout with the LA Lakers in 1971. According to legend, Hammond cooked future nine-time NBA champion Pat Riley in a one-on-one, impressed NBA single-season ppg record holder Wilt Chamberlain during a shooting drill, and was offered a contract. He hadn't even played HS or college ball. Hammond turned the funds down. He was earning more dough at the time living the street life.

That next season, the Lakers won a record-breaking thirty-three in a row and went 69–13 before the playoffs, then won the NBA Finals. That's how good they were. And they wanted to sign Joe Hammond. That's how good *he* was.

In 1978, the Destroyer scored seventy-three points at the Rucker. Not even four-time NBA scoring champ Kevin Durant, who in 2011 dropped sixty-six at an EBC game at '55th, could top Hammond's single-game high at the park.

Through the seventies and eighties, the Rucker continued to showcase a number of legends, too many to mention. In 1985, "Pookie" Wilson dropped seventy in a game there. Gerald "Dancing Doogie" Thomas would put on a show at '55th, too. He was king of what? King of styyyle! Aside from being the second-greatest backboard shooter Harlem's ever produced (after Joe Hammond, of course), Doog popularized what the hood called a "dip," a move he learned in the seventies by watching fellow Harlemite and NBA player Franklin Edwards. He would swing the ball back with one hand behind his head like he was about to bang it, then at the last second he'd bring it back forward for a sweet finger roll.

His signature layup became an identifier for uptown style, which in the nineties became known as "the butter roll," then in the 2000s "the jellyroll," and shortened these days to just "jelly," made world famous thanks to Isaiah Washington, the 2017 "Mr. New York Basketball" award winner for top HS player in the state. Washington's posts filmed on the courts north of 110th Street went viral on social. The roots of @jelly_dimes's millions of views started decades earlier with the influence of Doogie, a player who didn't even play HS ball. How amazing is the Harlem playground aesthetic?

In 1980, Greg Marius, a member of the rap group the Disco Four, debuted the Entertainer's Basketball Classic at Mt. Morris Park and attracted a thousand people on day one. "Greg G" moved the EBC to 1-3-9 and Lenox a few years later. Crowds would flock there to see "High Jumping" Artie Green, a ferocious dunker who once broke Ray Williams's nose because he boofed it so hard on the Knick guard's face. In a tight Whitney M. Young game, Artie fouled out with five minutes to go—and the stands completely cleared out! Harlem has always been thirsty for the show.

Alimoe

A couple of shorties who grew up watching the EBC, then played pickup at '39th as well as '45th Park up the block, wound up having a major impact on the game globally. Tyron "Alimoe" Evans became an international sensation when his highlights were featured in the AND1 Mixtape series. As a 6'7" point guard with crazy wiggles, it was a mystery to many how the "Black Widow" did not wind up in the NBA. Kareem Reid became a HS all-American who led St. Raymond's to city and state championships. The U. of Arkansas's all-time leader in assists also became *the* key player behind three consecutive chips from '02–'04 at '55th for Fat Joe's Terror Squad. God Shammgod also became a HS all-American, and made it to the league as a member of the Washington Wizards. His greatest contribution to the sport was a signature move he developed at night while trying to shake his own shadow up on Lenox. He unleashed "The Shammgod" on national TV in '97 against Arizona while reppin' Providence College in the

Shammgod

**HARLEM PLAYS THE BEST BALL IN THE WORLD**

NCAA Elite Eight. His defender moved five feet in the wrong direction off the whip-whop, and a new era in ballhandling was born. Every deceptive guard, including all-stars Chris Paul and Russell Westbrook, has included the push-out dribble to a snatch with the opposite hand into their repertoire since. And that all started in Harlem.

Rucker Pro League director Bob McCullough noticed that Greg Marius's tournament was outgrowing '39th and needed a larger space, so in 1987 he gave way to the new kid on the block and the EBC moved to Rucker Park. The who's who of the NBA and playground basketball have all played at '55th since, expanding the legacy of Mr. Holcombe Rucker's name throughout the world.

I've been blessed to play ball in forty-seven countries throughout six continents. No matter where I go, players always say, "I dream of one day playing at the Rucker." Other hoods can claim that they have a longer scroll of players in the NBA, but no one will argue that there is more history on the courts of Harlem than anywhere else. If Madison Square Garden is "The World's Most Famous Arena," then '55th is the equivalent for the outdoor game. Rucker Park is indeed the Mecca.

I moved from the LES to Harlem in May of 2004. On my first day as an official resident, instead of unpacking, I walked to Mt. Morris, where I'd had my first Holcombe Rucker Memorial game twenty-three years prior. Along the way I saw numerous kids working on their handles in front of their buildings. I saw two rollaway baskets, one in the courtyard of the projects on St. Nich, the other on the sidewalk around the corner. Basketball was inescapable. I was in my element.

Mt. Morris was popping with a crew on the pull-up bars, kids on the swings, and twenty-plus ballplayers spread out between the two courts. "How many people got next?" I asked. "About seven," a player who didn't look me in the face replied. On the sideline I saw "One-Eyed" Sam, who had coached a young Joe Hammond on this very court in the sixties. "These young kids don't know the game," a disgruntled Sam expressed. "They don't want to listen." I paid my respect, but I wasn't so sure I agreed with him.

Days later, I went back. "Al got next," a player revealed with indifference. Everyone seemed to know Al, so I asked him, "You got your five?" He shrugged me off as if I was bothering him. Just then a taller player walked up, and Al asked if he wanted to run. Big man wasn't interested, and I gave Al the *C'mon, b* face. He replied, "F it, you can run. I remember you." The difficulty of getting on a pound was not specific to Harlem. It was, and still is, one of the downsides to pickup. The upside is that it pushes you to play hard. You won't stay on the court that day or the next otherwise. Show and prove.

The game was a track meet with no D and two cherry pickers. I got some passes off that caught the attention of One-Eyed Sam's "young kids." They may have not been listening, but they were mos def watching. And they were instinctively yapping their jaws, too. A chorus

shouted, "Ooh, Ronnie, you got crossed!" One of our opponents was struggling to get buckets, so he got hit with, "Steve ain't got no handle!" No one had to train these teenagers how to critique style, or lack thereof. A player with wiggles is more revered in Harlem than anywhere else in the world. It's like dribbling a soccer ball for Brazilians. It's part of the socialization of adolescents.

Shannon Bobbitt, two-time NCAA champ

This has been the case since the 1960s. Ask Shannon Bobbitt, Renee Taylor, Crystal Bellinger, Niki Avery aka "The Model," Shammgod, Andre Blackett, Mike "Boogie" Thornton,

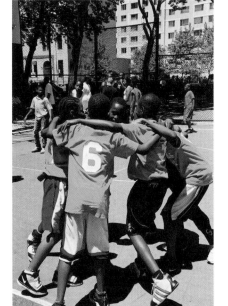

"Sudden" Sam Worthen, Ed Davis aka "The Sundance Kid," Arnold Dugger, Lonzo "Superkid" Jackson, Frank "Shake n Bake" Streety, Pablo Roberson, and countless other game-changing ball handlers/tricksters who have shocked and amazed crowds uptown.

Two mornings later, I went back to Mt. Morris to work on ballhandling drills. While crazy-diesel cats took turns doing dips on the bars, a homeboy in his early twenties asked me, "Are you that dude who was doing tricks the other day?" I said, "I don't know." Money replied, "My name's Kilo. A couple of kids were talking about you. I got something for you next time we play." I couldn't front—winning acceptance from a hyper-local Harlem audience that didn't know me from a can of paint meant more to me than when I performed at halftime with Project Playground in front of twenty thousand ticket holders in the Dallas Mavericks's arena.

This was Harlem, though, and accolades only endure as long as your last game, or take you as far as the park you've done damage at. The following week I ventured over to 118th and Morningside. There were only three heads watching a full. I asked, "Any of you have next?" A teenager replied, "I already got my five."

One-Eyed Sam was wrong. Young kids do understand the game, and they are continuing the legacy that is Harlem basketball where you don't get nothing for nothing. You get bizzy and earn your burn, or stay on the side courts to share your jumpers with prepubescents. The best ball is played here because of an unwritten law that every generation honors: *It started here. It ends here.*

Two hours later, the teammate at Morningside who gave me a chance to run changed his attitude toward me after he'd seen me play: "You were just what we needed tonight. That squad got so tired of losing, they quit . . ." Felt good to receive the love, but it didn't mean a thing when I wandered over to the next Harlem court and asked, "Pardon me . . . who got next?"

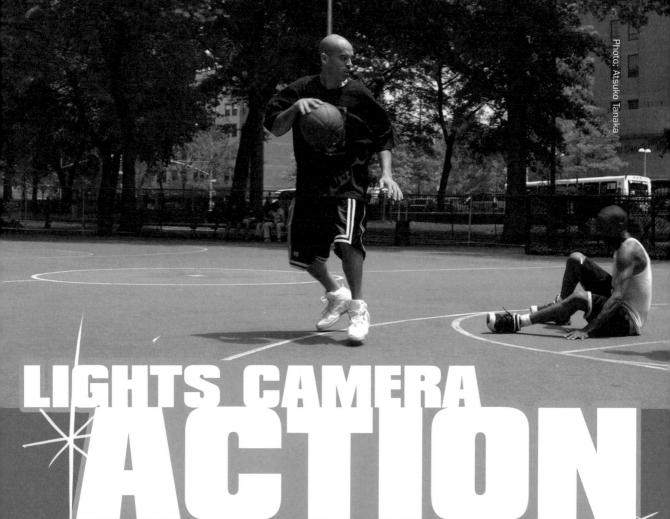

Photo: Atsuko Tanaka

# LIGHTS CAMERA ACTION

Before the summer of 2004 ended, I was playing 21 at Mt. Morris on a hot-ass afternoon until we had enough for a full. As sides were getting chosen up, this gray-haired viejo walked up to the court with green sweatpants tightly tied above his belly button. Both captains stopped in their tracks and asked, "Corky, you wanna run with us?" In my head I was like, *Who is this dude smoking a cigarette and getting so much attention?* A couple of plays in, wasn't hard to imagine why. The old man was agua from outside. Bang. Pump fake. Defender flew by. Another bang. Effortless. I kept feeding him. It was a hundred degrees and humid outside. We all looking like the dryer at the laundromat was out of order cuz our shirts were sopping wet, meanwhile Corky ain't even break a sweat. Game.

Afterward, Corky gave me a pound and said, "Good game, papa!" I returned the love, and then he asked, "How old are you?" I was about to turn thirty-eight, so he invited me to join him in the Pelham Fritz 38-and-over league in Harlem. "Tryouts for new players are in a few weeks, but listen—don't play well. I don't want someone else to see your skill set then pick you up. Don't worry. My squad is going to draft you. I give you my word. We can use a point guard like you with a handle who can also shoot . . ."

I showed up to IS 201 on 127th confused. Pelham Fritz was the premiere league in the city for baby boomers and Generation X, boasting players like 1979 NBA champion Gus "The Wizard" Williams, 1998 NBA assist leader Rod Strickland, 1972 USA Olympic Team member/former Indiana Pacer Mike Bantom, and 1988 Big East Conference Player of the Year/former New York Knick Charles Smith. The gym was also regularly packed with basically the Hall of

"Disco" Fred, "Corky," "Doogie," and "The Future"

Fame of Harlem. Mr. John Isaacs, Bob McCullough, Ernesto Morris, Pee Wee Kirkland, and Joe Hammond were regulars in the stands watching. "Master" Rob, "Speedy," "Dancing Doogie," "The Future," Steve "All Day" Burtt, and "Disco" Fred Brown battled on the court weekly. A.G. aka "The Voice of Harlem" was on the mic announcing. And . . . I'm supposed to hold back in front of an audience this power-packed?

A.G. got on the mic and bigged up my recruiter: "Corky Ortiz aka 'The Latin Assassin' is in the building . . ." I was like, *Oh sh\*t!* I hadn't realized my Mt. Morris teammate was the same Corky who was a legend at King Towers and the Schaeffer League, then got buckets in Puerto Rico's pro league, once dropping fifty-seven in a single game. And standing next to him was "Wil' Wild" Wes Correa, a former BSN MVP and champion on the island who once scored thirty-six points against Michael Jordan, Pat Ewing, and Chris Mullin of Team USA in a 1984 FIBA Americas game. If Corky envisioned me helping him and Wes out in the 38-and-over, then sh\*t, I was gonna do whatever I had to do. Which meant do nothing.

I was going through the motions during the scrimmage until Dexter Gardiner aka "Twin" crossed the cheerios out of my bunions then scored a fadeaway jumper, which caught an "Ooh!" from the crowd. Unwritten law in the hood states that if a player embarrasses you, you go right back at them on the very next play. And that's exactly what I did. I put a half spin on Twin at the T, pump-faked him into the air, then stepped through for a double-pump banker. Whistle blew. "Foul!" Hit the and-one. As I ran back on D, I looked at Corky dead in his eye and just shrugged my shoulders apologetically.

I joined Corky and Wes for the '04–'05 edition of Pelham Fritz. Halfway through the season, A.G. nicknamed me "Make It Happen." Dude was the hot announcer on the scene that year because Kingdome cooked up the summer prior. And just like all the greats before him, such as Gumby, Ronnie Green, Tango & Cash, Boobie Smooth, Joe Pope, etc., if your game wasn't correct, you'd hear that on full blast over the PA. A.G. didn't know nothing about my status in hip hop history or sneaker culture, so there was no bias. He showed me love strictly based on my game, and earning a nickname in Harlem literally made me a better player. Why? *Because I earned that sh\*t!*

In 2005, the Knicks produced the Last Man Standing one-on-one tournament in multiple locations throughout the tristate, and I qualified in Harlem to advance to Madison Square Garden for the final rounds. I was one of thirty-one ballplayers in the visitors' locker room on game day. I looked at each of the competitors, and I legit thought I had a chance to win. Field goals were worth one point, and behind the three-point line was worth two. I felt that was to my advantage. Everyone was feeling themselves and kinda giddy until Corey "Homicide" Williams entered the room . . . then things got real silent. The *New York Post* Summer Player of the Year had destroyed everyone in his path, bar none. The EBC at Rucker Park MVP was hungrier than anyone I'd ever seen play.

I won my first game and advanced to the round of sixteen, where I had to compete against AND1 Mixtape star Tim "Headache" Gittens. I did not want a repeat of when he'd embarrassed me at Ray Diaz a decade earlier, so even though me and him were like family, I put the only game face on, like if I was Big L on the mic about to black the f out up on me and Stretch's radio show in '95. My moms was at the Garden, too. That was the first time she had ever seen me play in my entire career. I had to represent.

Headache was taking me to the rack light status and went up 5–1. He had a hand in my face on all my jump shots. With his height advantage, I found it difficult to shoot over him, so I decided to pull from where he wouldn't expect me to—from three feet *behind* the NBA three-point line. I remember referee Eric Weaver, who was a friend of mine, saying, "That's from too far, Bob," as it left my hands. But *boom*. 5–3. Tim missed his next jumper; I got the rebound and sprinted right back to logo land. Splash. Tie game, b. 5–5! Headache had yet to shoot from deep, but on the next possession he went for the two-pointer . . . and hit it. Game.

As everyone expected, Corey Williams wound up indeed being the last man standing at MSG, and won the tournament. The future MVP of Australia's pro league knew me as the editor in chief of *Bounce Magazine*, and told me afterward, "I ain't know you could ball, too, old man." At a year shy of forty, I was the oldest player at the Garden that day—by a decade and change.

Although 2005 couldn't have gotten any better, I was straight trippin' when I was asked to be the host of ESPN's *It's the Shoes*, the first global TV series about kicks in broadcast history. Cocreators David Jacoby and Kevin Wildes, along with executive producer Jon Hock, had all read my book *Where'd You Get Those? NYC's Sneaker Culture, 1960–1987* and were inspired by it, so they invited my ideas for potential guests and segments. In the two seasons that we were on, I

interviewed Kobe Bryant, Spike Lee, Magic Johnson, Allen Iverson, Carmelo Anthony, Baron Davis, Fat Joe, Clark Kent, Biz Markie, Mr. Cartoon, and nearly every other personality from b-ball and hip hop that mattered in that era. I felt apprehensive about hosting a show that highlighted the collections of multimillionaire athletes and entertainers, though. A voice in my dome piece said, *You may appear to be promoting consumerism to a wide audience who doesn't understand the "why" of the movement.* So I suggested that we use the platform to give back to the community.

While I was the editor in chief at *Bounce*, I developed a great relationship with Hoops

4 Hope, a nonprofit based in South Africa and Zimbabwe that used basketball clinics plus donated sneakers from the US to draw youth, some of whom played shoeless, to their local centers, where they could learn about life skills and HIV prevention. So in my very first ESPN production meeting, I advocated that we feature H4H. Not only was the crew with it, but the head honcho Jon Hock also suggested we ask guests to autograph a pair of their own shoes to benefit our friends in the Motherland. From Missy Elliot to Trick Daddy on down, every celebrity cooperated. We gratefully collected some hot exclusives signed by the world's most famous, some of whom had grown up in poverty and could identify with not having comfortable grips to wear. At the end of the summer, Hoops 4 Hope held a fundraiser, auctioned off all the items, and raised thousands of dollars. We filmed the event, then aired a feature on the program during the season finale of *It's the Shoes*.

Courtesy of Hoops 4 Hope

Here's where the story gets trippy. A couple months later, Hoops 4 Hope founder Mark Crandall let me know that because of the TV exposure, people from all over the US had been organizing sneaker drives on behalf of the program. He and his directors on the ground decided to use the funds from the auction to build an outdoor b-ball center in Harare, Zimbabwe . . . dedicated in my name! I had to call last next at the local run in Harlem, yet at the same time there was a "Bobbito" court in my honor in Africa. Oooh-wee!

Courtesy of Hoops 4 Hope

I had momentum, just as if I was running a fast break downhill on uneven blacktop at Crack is Wack playground. I kept flowing with what the universe was putting in front of me . . .

I put hours in at Basketball City during the winter months. I got cool with a dude there who had a nice set shot and was the only other player wearing adidas Gil Zeros on the reg besides me. I always fed him the ball when we were on the same pickup squad, too. I had no clue that he was a VP for the Knicks, but one day, Dan Gladstone invited me to come to the Garden. In 2006, MSG Network wanted to launch *SummerBall*, the first TV series in the world solely dedicated to NYC's outdoor scene, and Dan told the VP of programming that I was the right person to host the show. I walked into the Penn Plaza office to meet the brass, who shared: "Everyone on the playground knows and respects you, Bobbito. You *are* the culture. We want you to be the personality that drives this. You don't even have to audition. It's yours if you want it . . ."

Mic drop.

On the first day of shooting, the producer handed me the very same stick mic with the MSG logo that legendary announcers Marv Albert and Clyde Frazier held during broadcasts for the Knicks. I was awestruck.

The hood ate the series up. I'd never been stopped on the street as much for anything I'd ever done. MSG showing reruns all week didn't hurt either. Even old ladies at my local bodega would tell me: "You the basketball guy, right? Love the show! Keep doin' your thing, baby . . ."

The most bizarre moment of it all was getting off a train at 34th Street and walking up to street level, then seeing the *SummerBall* on-air promo looping on the marquee screen above the Garden's entrance at Penn Station. I thought, *Thousands of people a day are seeing me do ball tricks while walking by the world's most famous arena.* It was effin' surreal.

The show's producer would always bug off on how much love, attention, and props I'd get in the streets. Turned out he also produced the Knicks broadcasts, so he asked if I'd do celebrity interviews at halftime during home games for the '06–'07 season. I wasn't a former NBA or even D1 player. At Wesleyan U. I studied sociology, not broadcasting. I was essentially making a jump from the playground to the pros, strictly based off the buzz all my years of hard work pounding the asphalt had created. Wooord.

On November 15, 2006, I made my debut as a member of the Knicks broadcast team during their game against the Wizards. I'm not gonna front—I was dumb nervous. On ESPN's *It's the Shoes*, we shot for forty-five minutes and then editors chopped it up to a flawless three-minute feature. My "Hot Minute at the Half" sideline report was live . . . at the Garden, where writers had newspaper columns expressly dedicated to critiquing us. There was nothing under-the-radar about it. Plus, there was the NBA corporate world of dress codes. Luckily, I didn't have to wear a suit, and I blew a sigh of relief when my first interviewee was Cam'ron, who I'd known since '93 when he was an unsigned artist named Killa Cam rhyming with Big L on me and Stretch's radio show.

I survived it. Announcers Gus Johnson and Kenny Smith both knew who I was and gave me warm welcomes and encouragement off camera. Al Trautwig unfortunately did not. The pregame/postgame commentator didn't even look me in my eye when he first shook my hand. I shrugged that negative energy off when Dan Gladstone introduced me to star guard Jamal Crawford in the locker room. Crawford said, "I know who Bobbito is . . . the dude with the crazy handle!" Then he gave me a pound and a homeboy hug. With that level of cosign from one of the deadliest ball handlers in league history, there was nothing anyone could tell me moving forward. I was good.

2006–'07 was an up-and-down season. The Knicks didn't make the playoffs and there was a lot of frustration from the fans when they'd lose, though I was able to enjoy the subtle brilliance of Jamal Crawford dropping a season-high fifty-two points one game from courtside. Being that close to the action allowed me to block out all the frenetic fan/media energy of the Garden. The sport started to appear just like it did on the block. I

Fat Joe photo: Alton Ritter

liked drawing the parallel. The NBA players were world-class professional athletes, but they were also the same people who any of us had lived next door to growing up. I didn't look at Stephon Marbury as the icon he was. The two-time all-star was on a stage much larger than I could ever comprehend, but in simple terms, he loved to hit a jumper, win a game, argue a call, and get some hot sneakers . . . just like me or anyone else who lived and breathed b-ball. He was a passionate human with complex feelings. He was a ballplayer. I felt like the rest of the world couldn't identify with the commonality, but should have.

01 4S

When I held down the "Hot Minute at the Half" in '06–'07, I became the first Latino member of the Knicks broadcast team in the sixty-year history of the franchise. I am not certain, but I may have been the first in league history, at least for English-speaking telecasts. It meant a lot to me personally. My father had passed ten years prior. He would've lost his sh*t seeing his son as a sideline reporter on the Garden floor.

# FINISH YOUR HOMEWORK

Photo: Stanley Lumax

I brought an authentic voice and/or on-camera presence to MSG Network's *SummerBall*, ESPN's *It's the Shoes*, EA Sports's *NBA Street* video games, and the plethora of work I did on behalf of Nike. In return, these same entities helped raise my status in the hood. I stood firm in mainstream corporate environments without having compromised myself whatsoever. I stayed true to the game. Kingdome's tournament director, Huncho, recognized that and knew I loved being on the mic, so he invited me to be the celebrity guest MC on their opening day in 2006. In the first couple of plays I called out, "He took it to the saucepan!"

and, "That was an airball dunk—finish your homework!" Legendary announcer Gumby told me at halftime, "You're funny!" That'd be like Jordan telling a kid, *You got hang time!*

I took that confidence with me to the big stage at the Rucker for the inaugural Elite 24 that went down September 1, 2006. To my knowledge, it was the first time a HS all-American game was being played outdoors—in the history of the sport. At first, the crowd was iffy about me. They were partial to the EBC announcers who had been there all summer, year in and year out, like Duke Tango, Al Cash,

Photo: Kelly Klinea

Hannibal, Boobie Smooth, and EJ the Mayor. Hannibal lived in the building directly across the street. EJ and his daughter played pickup there on Sunday mornings. They were embedded in the local matrix. I wasn't. I understood I had to earn their trust. I even got heckled in the first few minutes.

HERE, REP IS EARNED

LIK LIK SO UNIQUE
BLOCK PARTY
KEVLAR
THE MEDIC
FRESH PEPPER
E-Z PASS
BORN READY
GOOD TIMES
AMMO
DOO BE DOO
WIRELESS
PAY UP
REKE HAVOC
B-EASY
COLE PLAY

7TH ANNUAL
UNDER ARMOUR
elite 24

SATURDAY AUGUST 25 2012
THE TOP 24 HIGH SCHOOL BASKETBALL PLAYERS IN THE NATION
BATTLE IT OUT IN VENICE BEACH, CA

@UAELITE24
#ELITE24          LIVE ON ESPN U

UNDER ARMOUR      G      Wilson      Skullcandy

I broke the ice when I made a joke about my hairline, which had people rolling. Slowly, I won over the toughest audience in the world. The nicknames I was giving out certainly wasn't hurting, either. I called future 2010 NCAA Final Four Most Outstanding Player Kyle Singler "Wireless," which was dope and I could've left it at that, but he had long stringy hair that was flopping all over the place when he'd run, so then I donned him "The Wig." I heard people on all sides of the stands cackling, like, *Yooo!* The next time Kyle touched the rock, I nicknamed him "Shampoo," and said he was destined to have a lot of hair-care product endorsements. By that point, I was in with the crowd, and found my comfort zone to get even zanier on the mic. I nicknamed future NBA All-Star Kevin Love "Kevlar" cuz his rebounding and outlet passes were so strong, and hit future 2010 NBA Rookie of the Year Tyreke Evans with "Reke Havoc" cuz he made defenders look toy with his whip-whop handle.

My favorite tag of all was for Lance Stephenson. I had watched him play at Kingdome in the unlimited division the summer before his freshman year in high school. At the tender age of fourteen, Lance was already manhandling opponents who were grown-ass men. After he hit a seventy-five-foot buzzer-beater at the 2006 Elite 24, I shouted out, "That was Lance Stephenson aka 'Born Ready'!" Then I said, "Lance was born ready, peoples. He came out his mother's womb . . . in a defensive stance, yo!" Everybody fell out. Even Lance, who had his game face on, couldn't help but crack a smile.

Lance loved my nickname so much, he wrote *Born Ready* on his sneakers for the rest of his years at Lincoln HS, where he won an unprecedented four straight PSAL city titles and became the all-time leading scorer in state history.

The 2006 Elite 24 was insane for me to experience. I continued to announce the event through 2014. ESPN started televising it annually, and in 2010 I moved from the asphalt to on-camera talent for the network's broadcast. In front of millions of viewers or not, if I had a choice between being on the mic and being on the court playing, well . . . there was no contest. That's why the highlight of 2006— by far—was suiting up for the AND1 Mixtape Tour's first visit to my homeland Puerto Rico on September 16, just one week shy of my fortieth birthday. ESPN "Streetball" series star Aaron "AO" Owens invited me to run with them. I wasn't quite sure if he'd ever seen me play, though, other than the ballhandling tricks I'd done on *It's the Shoes* and the quick cameo I had in Mixtape Vol. 7 (where there was a clip of me doing my wraparound-the-chest no-look pass at a pickup run in SoHo). I wasn't trying to quiz him on why, though, and I'd surmise me being a recognized Boricua ballplayer/entertainer certainly didn't hurt.

**FINISH YOUR HOMEWORK**

I was invited to play in Mixtape Vol. 2 and like a big dummy passed. In 2004, I had gone to the open tryouts outside Madison Square Garden and almost made the cut to be in the building, but not quite. So finally having an opportunity to play in the AND1 Mixtape Tour that would be later broadcast on ESPN's *Global Invasion* series—in my homeland no less—with the most celebrated non-NBA players in the world at the time, was too lovely. I humbly accepted the offer.

A few weeks before the game, AND1 member Taurian Fontenette aka "Air Up There" threw down the first 720 dunk the world ever witnessed while the tour was in Houston. If you didn't pause for a second, then reread what I just wrote. Taurian legit did two 360 spins—in the air—then caught a clean woof to punctuate it. People didn't know that was possible. The highlight went viral, and the views went to infinity. Everyone was tuned in to see if he could repeat the feat. Everyone. And the show was coming to Puerto Rico.

The invite to be a part of the movement at its height felt almost absurd. The timing was just too good to be true.

It happened though. I arrived in Puerto Rico two days early con calma. As much as I loved eating pollo, arroz con habichuelas negras, y tostones, I straight kept my meals light, eating mostly salads with limited carbs, plus staying away from sweets for weeks leading up to the trip. I was gonna be the oldest player on either side—I had to be mentally and physically prepared.

*Global Invasion* producer Michael Kuhn asked if I could help introduce the AND1 players to my country, and of course I obliged. I brought them to las canchas de Lloren Torres (PR's largest housing projects) y La Perla. Michael kept asking me questions while I was being followed on camera, and I realized that the episode would be a bigger opportunity than just fulfilling a hoop dream. Once aired, I was going to provide the public with insight into the rich culture and history of La Isla del Encanto.

Game day rolled up, and I had a choice to run with AND1 or their opponents—the Puerto Rico Streetball All-Stars, whose members I had played against and bonded with during a 2005 tour I was a part of with other Nuyoricans like Headache. How was I gonna go against my own? I walked into the visitors' locker room and shouted out, "¡Lo dejó pegao!" and all my fellow Boricuas jumped up to give me a communal welcome. I'd made the right choice, though I was an unexpected extra body. There was only one uniform top left. The coach offered it to me, but I told him, "Nah, b, give it to one of the players from *here*." I went out on the court with my tank top undershirt on, straight up, on national television. Con orgullo.

Photo: Peyoweyo Rivera

I wound up guarding Andre Poole aka "Silk," who crossed the falafels out me twice—in the same play. *Oh!* I literally did a defensive slide in the wrong direction twice, like a toddler trying to mambo on mud. It happens. In the second half, I dribbled down, jumped in the air with my back to Silk, placed the ball on the floor and rolled it through my legs as well as his, then caught it on the other side and layed it for dos puntos. The Baltimore legend then came back and boomeranged it over my head while spinning at the same time. A couple of plays later, I ripped him.

Silk absolutely got the best of me, but for the record, I walked off the court with my head way up. He and I hugged after the game, and I told him, "B, a pleasure to have gone up against you." He replied, "Ah, man—mad respect to you, Bobbito!" Real classy brother. Right afterward, AND1 team captain "Main Event" jumped in front of the camera and pointed at me, saying, "Stretch and Bobbito . . . I used to listen to them back in the day!" The love was thick, and I was humbled by it all.

**FINISH YOUR HOMEWORK**

As if the night couldn't have gotten better, after the game the crowd sprawled across the brand-new wood floor at El Coliseo, and Air Up There did his 720 dunk in front of everyone. I still can't quite figure out how that yoke was physically possible. And I'm unaware of anyone else successfully pulling it off since. Frozen moment in b-ball history, basically. And I was *there*, saw it with my own eyes.

After the *Global Invasion* episode aired on ESPN, I got so much positive feedback, particularly from mi gente. I was DJing one night at the Candela Bar in Viejo San Juan, and this Boricua rolled up behind the turntables to embrace me. After a long hug, he shared, "Thank you for raising our people up and making us look so good." I caught goose bumps. His words hit me right in my heart, especially since I had struggled in my youth identifying as a Puerto Rican not born on the island.

When I got back to New York shortly after, I was at a bodega in El Barrio where

Photographer unknown

a Drake's Cakes driver recognized me from *Global Invasion*, too, and got so amped he offered me a free case of Ring Dings. My eleven-year-old heart wanted to yell, *Hell yeah!* but I humbly declined. That's how my peoples do, though.

Madrid Photos: Kevin Couliau

ARRIVAL

PASSPORT STAMPS

KOOL BOB LOVE
24

Being on TV was exhilarating, but simply playing pickup in Harlem fed the core of my soul. I went from park to park in a manner that was very present, and in the moment. I did not own a cell phone and was completely unreachable while at the court. To say I had peace of mind would be an understatement. Being disconnected allowed me to be *truly* connected to the kids, teenagers, and young adults I balled with, some of whom looked up to me. What we shared was mutually uplifting.

During these same years from '05–'09, I was flying around the world like an arctic tern. I'd literally be on the road three to four weekends out of every month, and would have to renew my passport every two years because I'd run out of blank pages for customs to stamp. Most of these trips were DJ gigs. I'd arrive, take a nap, then ask the local promoter if they knew where cats played pickup so I could get a sweat in before the event jumped off. I searched for runs, though they weren't always easily found.

The first time I balled in Paris after a gig, I traveled an hour and a half by train and bus—plus got lost—just to find Île de Puteaux. Vale la pena. *Bounce Magazine* contributing photographer Kevin Couliau brought down Ibrahim Koudié from the Carquefou pro club, and the three of us won all night. A pro from Belgium got real tight with all the Ls, so he challenged me one-on-one. I had him at point, but he came back to beat me, all the while talking mad smack in French (which I don't speak a lick). I don't think I would've encountered that brashness in the nineties. Normally just being from New York would've intimidated opponents, but the rest of the world had caught up. I was down with that. Helps the game continue to expand.

01 53

DJ Typhoon booked me to spin in Denmark fourteen times, and I dead-ass thought about moving to Copenhagen part-time. I just loved how their society operated. There were no prisons, no unhoused population, and the overall vibe, at least on the surface, seemed chill. On one visit, Typhoon's boy Benji, a member of the national team, took me to an outdoor court where women were topless on the sideline left and right. I was like, *How am I supposed to concentrate here?!* All the best players mostly ran indoors, so the next day we hit a gym that smelled like a NYC nightclub before the smoking ban. Bleh. Benji and I went at each other all night, though. He tried to Shammgod me! Afterward, my new buddy offered to trade a pair of his game shorts for my Ham Fish tournament T-shirt. Clearly, I got the best of the deal, but for him, owning anything from NYC's fabled scene was a steal. So I guess it was a fair foreign exchange.

When I spun in Stockholm for the first time, the promoter DJ Mad Mats struggled to find a run for me, so we went old school and broke into a gym. Mats corralled a few teenagers, one of whom was stupid nice with a handle, jumper, and hops. The kid loved the game but hated being restricted by coaches, so he had turned down an offer to go pro in the Swedish league. I understood his decision, but he could've been the man for the local club called the Stockholm Human Rights. That's gotta be the flyest name for a team ever. I could've traded another one of my little-known-NYC-tournament shirts for his game shorts. Dag!

I DJed a bunch in London during these years as well, though struggled to locate an outdoor run. I'd find courts where they had fútbol goals under the b-ball rim. I'd be like, *What the f?* Luckily, I became tight with Nhamo Shire, who was a player and part owner of the Westminster Warriors pro club, so he'd always open the gym for us, then make the mistake of challenging me to a three-point shootout. I'd talk smack, like, "B, I'm on your home court, jet-lagged with jelly in my legs, and you still can't beat me?" We'd laugh for hours. What a beautiful bond that can be formed internationally through this game.

When DJ Spinna and I took our "Wonder-full" Stevie Wonder tribute party to the Bay Area for the first time, the Oakland legend of legends Demetrius "Hook" Mitchell arranged an invite-only run for me. There were no slouches there—even the youngest players wore shirts that read, *Northern Cal Top 100*. At 5'9", Hook caught national attention in the nineties by jumping over cars and motorcycles in dunk contests that he'd win easily, but what impressed me most in person was how he passed unselfishly and moved without the ball. It was clear why NBA All-Stars Gary Payton and Jason Kidd regarded his game so highly. Truthfully, his jumper had better mechanics and accuracy than either of them, from what I witnessed that day. Unfortunately, the Bay Area point god wound up in state prison, never fully realizing his potential as a ballplayer during his prime. Similar to Earl Manigault's story, though, Hook dedicated a lot of his time toward mentoring the next generation once he got out so that they wouldn't fall into the same traps he did. Good brother and was wonderful meeting such a force.

**PASSPORT STAMPS**

In very few instances, I got booked overseas to DJ, play ball, *and* be a sneaker personality. 2007 marked the twenty-fifth anniversary of Nike's Air Force 1 model, and the Swoosh hired me to be a triple-threat "ambassador" for the celebration cuz my history went so deep with the iconic shoe. I designed three low-cuts and four high-tops with hits of my nickname and image, with colors and fabrics inspired by my ties to b-ball and hip hop. Art director Al Baik created a logo for these kicks with a hand over a 12" record, and another with the same hand over a ball. *¡Salsa picante!* My curated collection was released right alongside silhouettes featuring the original 1983 AF1 endorsees, including NBA champions Michael Cooper, Moses Malone, Bobby Jones, and Jamaal Wilkes. Parties in NYC, Las Vegas, Toronto, Beijing, and Hong Kong followed, and I was flown to each town to spin vinyl, host Q&As, and do endless press interviews. All these trips were memorable, but my excursion to Tokyo was life-defining.

My first visit to the "Land of the Rising Sun" had been with Stretch in '95. Our radio show was making waves on the other side of the world, so much so that I saw forty mixtapes for sale with our name on the spine at a record shop—directly behind the register in prime real estate. We weren't manufacturing them ourselves yet; the power of our broadcasts made them valuable enough to be bootlegged. While shopping, I found super-exclusive kicks that I'd never seen stateside before, or since. The promoter wouldn't let me pay for anything. They were the consummate hosts.

The only thing missing was the chance to play ball. In 1999, Japan, with a population of over one hundred million,

only had twenty-five outdoor courts—in the entire country. I met players who set up mobile backboards in parking lots and empty buildings. The passion was thick and they made it happen. When I produced/directed my *Bobbito's Basics to Boogie* instructional DVD in 2003, a local distributor picked up the rights to release a subtitled version domestically. Japan was the first foreign-language nation to license it. I had already felt the love from their dance community at the clubs I'd rocked, so I welcomed receiving the same from b-ball devotees.

That all went next level in May of 2007. Nike and the 1 Love shop organized the Bobbito in Tokyo: Hoops-Kicks-Beats from NYC Tour. Straight bananas. I was picked up at the airport by a stretch limo that had my name and likeness decaled on the door. WHAAAT?! I was like, *Do I deserve this?* The next forty-eight hours were a blur . . .

First stop was the Ueno shopping area. I met a store owner who proudly boasted, "I was the first account to carry Air Force 1s in Japan!" His shop was reminiscent of the golden days of digging for kicks on Delancey Street, even smelled like it. That evening I spun records at Club ageHa in front of 4,500, which was the largest indoor crowd I ever had in my DJ career. I tried tallying the number of speakers in the room . . . and lost count. The legendary DJ Muro was on the bill as well. I'm glad I didn't have to go on after him. The "King of Digging" shut the place down when he pulled out doubles of the Jungle Brothers's "Because I Got It Like That"

on 7". I had never seen it pressed up as a 45. Maybe he had the only two copies in the world? I was flummoxed.

The next day was truly bonkaroonies. Nike and *ALL-DAY Magazine* put together a "Dream Game" exhibition at Yoyogi Park, featuring the country's top pro and playground players. 1,500 people showed up to watch, which was the biggest crowd for an outdoor basketball game in Japanese history. When I rolled up, kids were waiting outside my car for photos and autographs. I thought, *This must be how the AND1 Mixtape cats be feeling on tour.* I was straight tripping—in the very best way.

I was also physically exhausted from the thirteen-hour time difference, the DJ gig, the interviews, the rigid itinerary of appearances, and the overall lack of downtime, but the universe smiled upon me. Immediately after tip-off, I hit my first four jumpers, all from behind the NBA three-point line. I had to chase local trickster Tana Wizard on D, though, and he cracked me bad one play with a crossover through my legs which I swiped at but missed. I went right back at him the next play and dribbled the ball around his back, then pulled, but my jumper didn't connect to complete the highlight. The announcer, Mamushi, hyped up our back-and-forth to the crowd with his play-by-play, and a DJ threw down underground hip hop joints from the nineties during time-outs. There I was on the other side of the globe, feeling like I was back home.

During halftime, trick freestylers Block & Lock performed the tightest group routines I'd ever seen. They told the crowd that me, Jack Ryan, Ramón Rodríguez, and Kenny Rodriguez's Project Playground performances had influenced them, so they invited me to join the circle. I went out and did some juggling and two-ball butters. The audience went absolutely bonkers.

My top highlight in the second half was putting my man on a butter puddle when he stumbled from an in-and-out-screeeeech-halt-step-back bong-bong I whipped on him. I missed the shot afterward, but the crowd didn't care; they howled for me anyway.

I finished the game shooting 50 percent from the field, though my squad lost on a buzzer-beater three-pointer directly in my grill piece. I had to remind myself what a teammate in Harlem once told me: "Bob, you're forty. You're exempt from playing D the rest of your life. Just shoot threes!" After the game, mad people were asking for more photos, autographs, my uniform, sneakers, a hug, you name it.

On the ride back to the hotel, I rolled down my window to wave back to the kids cheering for me by the park exit. Then it hit me. I had picked up a ball when I was seven, and dedicated a lifetime to the game. I could have never fathomed I'd one day design a pair of sneakers for Nike, much less the number-one-selling reissued model in their brand's history. My DJ career had started in the nineties on a tiny hundred-watt college radio station. No way could I have anticipated I'd eventually be drawing large crowds to hear me spin at clubs on the other side of the world. Not in my wildest dreams could I have imagined

that one day I'd inspire ballplayers on a global level, but since I'd never stopped striving toward expanding my creative muscle, even as I hit my forties, I somehow went beyond everyone's expectations—even my own.

My b-ball/kicks/beats footprint materialized hard body in Japan that trip. And what a blessing it all was. I was so overwhelmed with the realization, I took a deep breath, allowed my chest to expand, and as I exhaled, my eyes got watery.

The cool Japanese wind coming through the window gave me a soft hug. On that bright afternoon, I sensed my body rising off the land toward the sun.

All the traveling domestically and internationally was a thrill, but at the same time took a toll on my body. I moved at a high-functioning gear, though. When I got back from the Japan tour one Sunday afternoon, I went straight to my tub for a twenty-minute hot bath, then literally raced out the door so I could be on time for warm-ups at my SBL game inside West Side HS on 101st Street. My teammates were shocked that I even showed up. They were like, "Weren't you in Tokyo *this morning*?" Yet I cherished every moment I could get on the court, most especially in New York, so I stretched and got my burn. Life starts today, every day.

May 20, 2009, was destined to be hectic. I was packing records for a DJ mini tour on the West Coast: five gigs, four cities, five consecutive nights. I had flyers for an upcoming local event that I wanted to drop off at the Vault sneaker shop on 133rd, and en route, I passed by the old Rucker on 130th and Seventh. Three cats were playing 21. I slowed my bike-pedal cadence down so I could mosey on by. I was tempted to stop and play, but I knew it would cost me invaluable time. I kept it moving.

On my way back, the 21 was still going on. I rolled over the faintly painted edge of the court to watch for a sec. Two of the three players had skills. It was always difficult to find decent comp outdoors at twelve thirty in the afternoon. I was getting tempted. Between the sh*tload of work I had to knock out and the fact that I was rocking canvas Super PRO-Keds (once a mighty ball shoe in the seventies but long since eclipsed for performance), I had enough cause to resist. I kept saying in my head, *You don't have time. Don't do it. Don't . . .*

"Yo, Bobbito, you playing?" Jalani asked from the opposite side of the fence as he walked up. I had coached him at Basketball City's youth camp when he was a preteen and hadn't seen dude in a minute. Now he was a young man with a physique. He said, "I came out to do ballhandling drills."

"Yeah, I'll jump in," I responded. I had to at that point.

"If you gonna play, then I will too," Jalani decided.

I wasn't stretched, hadn't eaten yet, was looking like a throwback Rock Steady Crew b-boy from 1977 in my canvas high-tops, but I found myself stepping on the court, asking, "Who got the high?"

"I got ten," declared big man in the tournament-I'd-never-heard-of T-shirt. Second high belonged to I-just-finished-doing-225-sets-of-pull-ups/sit-ups man. The third participant—I wouldn't exactly qualify him as a player—had on jeans and looked like he'd snuck out his job for lunch. "Let's start a new game, though," big man announced as Jalani and I both joined.

I figured I'd warm up by playing hard D. On Jalani's first possession, he went right at my jugular. With a quick jab step to a double crossover, finishing with the left, it was immediately apparent that his game had vastly improved, and that he wanted me to know it. Cool. What was a casual game before we showed up had just become a doozy. The ball rolled out of bounds, and we both hustled for it. He practically dove into the fence to beat me to the rock. I asked if he was alright, and big man snorted, "He a'ight. That's nothing; Jalani be *skateboarding*! Ha ha!"

"Nice move, Bob," Jalani grunted after I had thrown the ball in front of me, tapped my right foot with my left hand with a hop jump, then stepped back to hit a geezer. I was finally warming up. No way did I want to take an L to a shorty I once coached at camp. He was always a friendly kid to me, though. While Super Sit-Up Man took a foul shot, Jalani asked me, "What was Big L like? I heard the freestyle with Jay-Z he did on you and Stretch's old radio show . . ."

It was interesting that he was asking about Big L. The last time I saw L alive had been at this very court in the nineties. I had a game in the Byrd's Classic against hip hop legend Lovebug Starski's squad, then afterward we all shot around for a while and kicked it. As ferocious as L was on the mic while dropping verses, I found him to be a quiet, keep-to-himself-type cat otherwise. And always showing me love. When I'd heard he allegedly got shot in his face on 1-3-9 and Lenox, my body cringed. He didn't survive the streets that he rhymed about, but the recordings of his appearances on me and Stretch's WKCR radio program have endured. The nine-minute freestyle of L and Jay-Z on our show from 1995 might possibly be the most-listened-to live recorded moment in hip hop history. Period.

"Big L was so focused when he'd kick a verse, he'd black out on the mic. When we were off the air in the studio, he was cool as a cucumber slice."

After big man heard me speak, he offered, "Anyone ever tell you you sound just like that dude from *NBA Street*?"

"That's me," I replied.

The next play, I went between the legs to a front crossover whip-whop bong-bong on him and finished with a floater over everyone else's outstretched arms. He said, "Hmm, that was fast like 500,000 million." I couldn't help but smile at the compliment.

I had high and was drawing double teams every possession now. On one play, I waved my hand between 1,000 Pull-ups's ankles. He didn't flinch, so I then threw the ball through his legs, caught it on the other side, and dipped it for two. A couple of cats crept up to watch and joined big man in announcing the highlights. Jalani was guarding me thirty feet from the basket, and I did an inside hand change behind his back, which he half bit, then I went hard left, crossed back under my leg, and banged a twenty-three-footer, HONG.

"You got mixed, Jalani," the sideline screamed, "and he got on PRO-Keds! Ha ha!"

It was anyone's game. Jeans man had decided to take a break and sit down. He was on his donut when he jumped back in. As awkward as his game was, before I knew it, duke was two points behind me with sixteen. Never underestimate anyone who looks like a burger.

I needed to finish this game and get moving, so I killed the yo-yo strings and went straight basic, got to twenty, then hit the twenty-three-footer to put it in the can. "Run it!" big man said authoritatively. By unwritten playground law, it's mad rude to visit someone's home court, get a quick W, and not give them the op for revenge.

"I gotta be out, yo," I blurted regretfully, knowing that I'd had so much bananas fun I didn't really want to leave. But I had to. "I'll be back."

Five days later, I returned from my DJ mini tour. I went straight from JFK to the crib to drop my record bag off, then darted to link with my boy Elliot Peter Curtis who was in town visiting. He'd never played ball uptown, so we met at the Goat for a one-on-one. Early in the first game, I assumed my usual defensive squat, and EPC jab-stepped right, then ran his arms with the ball across his chest to go left . . . BAKATA! His elbow inadvertently clocked my forehead. My head felt like a dinging bell from a boxing ring, and my flesh had split open. How much so I had no idea, but by virtue of watching my blood spill onto my K1X tee like a cherry piragua bottle had exploded, I figured it had to be bad.

"Bob, I'm *so* sorry . . ."

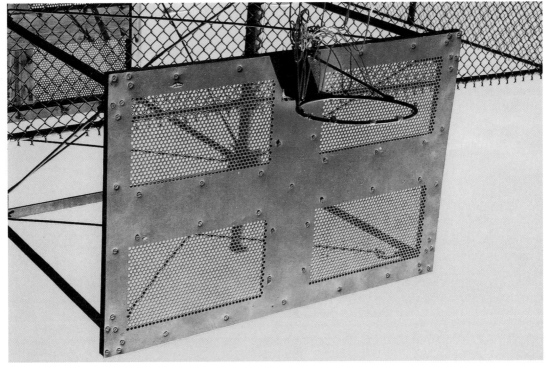

Elliot had no intention. The Massachusetts native was a good kid, and had just graduated from Carnegie Mellon where he created the first ever higher learning course on sneaker culture. His class used my *Where'd You Get Those? New York City's Sneaker Culture: 1960–1987* as the main text!

"You're gonna need stitches, bro," a homeboy advised as he handed me some paper towels from the Parks & Rec hut. "I see you still out here doin' it, b—that's fly. The last time I saw you, you gave my big brother the bizness. Keep it up, fams."

The bleeding wasn't stopping, trickling onto my new Lebron VI U. of Akron exclusives, which got wrecked. Wasn't really concerned at that point. I had Elliot gather my stuff, then noticed that the teenagers playing three-on-three on the next court had stopped and were all staring. As we walked out the Goat, Elliot told me nervously, "I don't think those kids were too happy I did that to you. I'm lucky to have walked out of here alive." I reassured him that it wasn't his fault—that's what I got for trying to play hard D in my forties!

Walking toward Broadway to catch a cab, I finally peeped the wound in a car's door mirror. The gash was deep and almost a half inch wide. I could've gone to the emergency room and paid two thousand dollars to get stitches, but instead I decided to wait till the next morning to get patched at my primary doctor's office for a couple hundred.

Bad move.

A dear friend came over to my crib and riffed with me for an hour about going to ER. I should've listened, but I was stubborn. We changed my bandage every hour because the wound would not stop bleeding until just before I went to bed.

The next morning, I woke up feeling groggy. I was physically exhausted, had lost a lot of blood, and didn't drink enough water the night before. As we changed my bandage, I . . .

"Bob! Bob! Are you alright?"

I laid on the ground of my kitchen, not knowing how I'd gotten there. I had fainted and landed headfirst, which was supposedly how my father died. I looked down and saw a pool of burgundy puddles on top of my cherrywood floor. I thought my gash from the day before had opened again. I had no idea that I had just caught a new one, quadruple the size, above my left eyebrow.

Homegirl could see my skull as she held gauze up to the flesh that was hanging toward my cheekbone. She didn't want to alarm me so didn't share how bad it looked. I was bleeding profusely and feeling lightheaded again. When the ambulance showed up, I told the paramedics repeatedly, "I'm okay, I'm okay." I had no idea.

Truthfully, I really did feel fine. I guess my body was in shock so my nervous system shut down. I was rushed to St. Luke's Hospital on 114th Street, the same place I was born, had my tonsils plus appendix removed, caught four stitches in my forehead after I crashed through a glass coffee table, and where I'd had my first knee operation. That all happened before I was eleven years old—I grew up as no stranger to the operating room.

Gracias a la energía universal, the CAT scan showed no signs of internal bleeding, fracture, or concussion. I did catch thirty-five stitches between the lacerations and contusion I suffered to the grill piece. The doctor told me I couldn't play ball until further notice. That might've hurt the most. All the summer tournaments were starting the following week.

It was a costly elbow.

I returned home that evening, and in the middle of the night, I started twitching in bed. It alarmed my friend, so she woke me up by softly shaking my shoulder. "Bob, are you okay?"

I replied, "I was trying to touch the rim . . ." and then fell right back to sleep.

The next morning when I woke up, I couldn't recall saying that—at all.

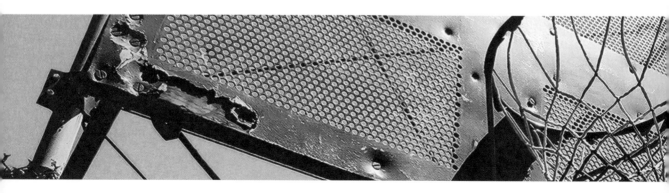

Weeks passed, and by mid-June I was cleared to step back on the court. My boy Roman Perez asked me to run with him at West 4th. I had been mentoring him since we first played against each other in 2005 at Rodney Park. I gave him twenty-five, he asked for my number after the game, and we've been tight ever since. Roman reminds me so much of myself when I was his age it's ridiculous. We're kindred b-ball spirits. I had to really consider whether I was up for playing at "The Cage" under the whistle, though. I was coming off my blackout, and was months from turning forty-three. I knew it would mean a lot to mi hermanito, though, so . . . I accepted. Surprised? (By this point in the book, you already knew what I'd decide, ha ha!)

I first played in West 4th during the nineties for "Panama," then legendary United Brooklyn coach Sid Jones, and was a role player on each squad. I made small contributions off the bench, and was just happy to get a shirt, the classic drawstring bag, and be a part of the environment. Since 1977, that tournament has been a consistent staple for both the men's and women's b-ball communities of New York, with a who's who roster of players including "Fly" Williams, "Sudden" Sam Worthen, Mario Elie, "Dancing Doogie," Jack Ryan, Anthony Mason, "Speedy" Williams, Conrad McRae, "Smush" Parker, Janice Thomas, Renee Taylor, WNBA champion Epiphanny Prince, and too many others to mention.

When I was an assistant coach at John Jay College, I put our ladies squad at the Cage for the summer so they could go against the best comp possible. When we played against future WNBA All-Star and champion Essence Carson, I was in awe of her game. What I found most impressive about that season, though, was the camaraderie across the board—not just among individual teams, but between *everyone* there, from the announcer to crowd members to the scorekeepers and beyond. Women's outdoor basketball in New York may not have caught as much attention as the men's in the past, but there was a vibe that resonated on a higher plane within that community. I was blessed to witness it for that short time.

While the West 4th tournament has an amazing legacy, pickup basketball there may quite possibly have an even loftier status. The Cage is arguably the most coveted asphalt in the world for players outside of organized ball to showcase their skills. Playing there is almost a rite of passage. When Nate Robinson was a rookie with the Knicks, he showed up one afternoon and ran a full—*during* the season. Other stars from the NBA have been drawn to lace up alongside the park regulars over the summers, including fan favorites Baron Davis, Brandon Jennings, Pat Beverley, on and on. The comp may not be elite every single day, but the atmosphere has always been unmatched.

I hadn't played in the tournament since '97, yet I was still very familiar with the Cage as I'd pop in over the years for pickup. Sherm "Ice" was the mayor and everything ran through him. "Doc," "Butta," "Rock," and Mel "Murda" were his boys and the park regulars who could snap. Sometimes there'd be just as much of a crowd on the fence for the five-on-five as there was for their jokes.

01 67

The Future

One day, Malloy "The Future" Nesmith and I wound up on the same squad. We had also been teammates in the Darby's All-Star Classic #40over at the Kennedy Center uptown, where we averaged a combined forty-five ppg as a backcourt one season. We had point, and Malloy dribbled past his defender at the top of the key. He could've shot, and would've hit the dagger I'm sure, but instead he dimed me on the wing outside the three-point line.

Bang! I nailed that jumper as if his pass was a master's degree. In his prime, Malloy had NBA potential with serious talent. The fact that the legend respected my game to the point where he'd *entrust* me to keep us on the court . . . felt like a graduation.

I took that jewel with me to the 2009 West 4th Street tournament. Early in the season, we faced U. of Florida star PG Erving Walker. Former LA Laker Smush Parker grew up playing at the Cage, and was on the fence watching. Neither of them had ever seen me play. I got amped and wanted to show them a lil' something. Off the opening tip, the ball landed in my hands. I was literally a step in from half-court, and without thinking twice I pulled. Splash. Okay, that was a nice way to make a statement. Not to be outdone, Walker came right back at me and nailed a three from twenty-five feet out. I hit my next two treys then a runner, and finished the first quarter with eleven points on 80 percent shooting from the field. Then unselfishly, I subbed myself out. Roman had younger guys on the squad. I didn't want to take playing time away from them, and we needed fresh legs on D (I surely wasn't our top defender). Besides, I knew I couldn't keep up that scoring pace with Walker, whose squad went on to blow us out by the end of the game. Afterward, Smush gave me dap. I was *strillsnaight*.

Roman's heart was bigger than the collective height of our team. We took Ls left and right, and I became the de facto player/coach to keep morale up. In the middle of the season, I caught a steal plus hit two clutch threes in the last two minutes to lock our second win. Afterward, West 4th Street acting director Rick Johnson asked me, "You busy next Wednesday?" I was thinking he wanted me to DJ an event for them. "You got selected to the all-star game . . ."

I'd never been invited to an all-star game in a major tournament—but for that to happen in my forties?

Wednesday rolled up, and the park was packed. In crunch time, I hit a deep three a step in from half-court to tie the game 90–up and felt the crowd's cheers on my neck hairs. On our next possession, I got my man off-balance with a pump fake in the lane, then scooped my layup off the bank before the help D shifted over. That put us in the lead permanently. Heads on the fence went bonkers. My whole body swarmed with adrenaline. Like I felt that sh*t in my *soul*. All this after catching thirty-five stitches in my forehead and missing three weeks in June . . .

I felt truly blessed to be alive, healthy, and living life exactly how I wanted to—playing ball. In recognition, I decided to finally visit Dad's grave for the first time since he was buried back in 1997. I really felt his presence and was moved by it all. I told him that his son was doing alright. I knew he was proud.

Photo: Kevin Couliau

★ BOBBITO'S BOOK OF B-BALL BONG BONG

REFLECTION ETERNAL

Photos: Brian Benjamin

Coaching Roman's squad at West 4th cemented our friendship for life. The experience felt similar to when I coached at El Puente HS for Peace and Justice in Williamsburg, Brooklyn, the winter of '96–'97. The small public school run by a nonprofit had sixty-plus boys enrolled, twenty of whom showed up to tryouts, but only six were academically eligible. I didn't have to cut anyone. We didn't have our own gym, so after classes I'd walk them to another high school's facilities a mile and change away for practice. With no home court, we played all our games on the road, and won only once the entire season.

With both Roman's West 4th crew and El Puente's varsity squad, my coaching ethos was the same that I applied to myself when I was a teenager: *It's not whether you win or lose, it's how you play the game.* My high school kids played their hearts out every time on the floor, and even with a 1–20 record, they walked out each opponent's gym with their heads up. With everything going on in their lives, trust me, that was worthy of admiration.

When El Puente was founded in the 1980s by former Young Lords Party member/ Puerto Rican activist Luis Garden Acosta, Williamsburg simultaneously had the highest rates for murders and high school dropouts in the city. At the time I got hired, the community was fighting environmental racism because garbage dumps were being built just blocks away from the building. One of my players was living with his grandparents in the projects because his single parent had died of AIDS. One by one, they'd reveal layers of their daily realities, and I'd listen. I couldn't distance myself as someone designated to just teach them basketball. I became their coach, mentor, and to their surprise and delight, their bug-out buddy. They needed some light moments. On a train ride up to the BX one day, I noticed a passenger dead-sleep snoring with his mouth open. I told the squad, "Look at your mans," and we all fell out laughing.

01 71

In 2010, the SEED Academy in Senegal partnered with the US State Department to create the "Grow the Game" initiative, and founder Amadou Gallo Fall's team invited me to give skill clinics in five cities: Dakar, Thiès, Saint-Louis, Louga, and Linguére. They had absolutely no knowledge of my past coaching stints. The welcome was based on my contributions to outdoor b-ball culture in New York. It was as if I had created the opportunity from the karma of giving back to my community for so many years with all the undocumented hours I'd spent teaching lil' kids proper shooting form or dribble moves uptown and beyond.

Upon arrival in Dakar and before I even touched a ball, SEED director Brian Benjamin invited me to visit Gorée Island. I'd never heard of it. As soon as I got off the ferry, a street vendor getting his hustle on selling the native kesng kesng instrument looked at me and said, "Hola, primo. ¿Cómo estás?" He caught me off guard in the kindest way. I hit him back with, "¿Cómo sabes que yo soy Boricua?"

"I used to live in Harlem. I can tell you're from there. My name's Mika . . ."

"Maa ngi tudd Bobbito. Na nga def . . ."

"Wait . . . how you speak Wolof?"

When me and Stretch were on the radio in the nineties, there was a Senegalese cabdriver named Rahim who would call up the show at five a.m. We would put him live on the air and he'd always shout out his wife and daughters back on the continent. Dude was doing twelve-hour shifts six days a week to send money to his loved ones. One night, I asked him if he could pick me up when we signed off. Five minutes later, his yellow taxi was outside the station waiting for me. Beautiful soul. Rahim and I then become boys. I'd ride in the front seat while he'd pick up other passengers. We'd listen to hip hop tapes to tune out the dumb conversations in the backseat. He told me NBA All-Star Jayson Williams from the Nets once gave him a hundred-dollar tip for a trip that was only five bucks on the meter. Other than that, the norm was indifference, or sometimes disrespect, from his riders. Rahim lit up when I asked if he could teach me basic Wolof words like *hello, goodbye,* and *thank you*. My block in Harlem was called "Little Africa." The least I could do was greet him and our fellow neighbors from his country respectfully.

"Would you like to see the Door of No Return? C'mon, I'll take you . . ."

Mika got on his crutches and guided me up a steep hill. The Door was centuries old, and the last piece of Africa many enslaved people from the continent would touch. I could literally see the scratches, and maybe blood, that were still on the concrete doorframe, and my head imagined the horror of attempting to resist leaving one's homeland against one's will, only to get forced onto a ship bound for hell.

Basketball was taking me to parts of the world where I could experience history in a manner I may not have ever encountered otherwise.

"Jërëjëf, Mika. Take down my number, fam. When you come back to Harlem, hit me up. I gotchu . . ."

Our first "Grow the Game" clinic was in Linguére. Fifty kids showed up, one of whom was a 6'11" sixteen-year-old. I started leading the group through drills, and this tall-ass teenager was shining. A San Antonio Spurs scout was part of our staff, and he told me, "Shorty wasn't on our radar." I gave him the *Huh?* face, so he continued: "There's only about fifty seven-footers born in the world every year, and we're pretty much aware of all of them. If they wind up interested and skilled in basketball, then they become an NBA prospect. We'll get this kid into the SEED Academy. It'll open up doors for him . . ."

Since 2002, SEED has provided intense academic and basketball training to thousands of youth with the goal of developing the next generation of leaders, in a country that is not traditionally known for b-ball and had four indoor courts total when I visited. Only a third of Senegal's students attend high school, and less than 10 percent go to college. In contrast, over 90 percent of SEED's graduates further their education at universities or secure a job upon program completion, almost 60 have received athletic scholarships in the US, and a handful have made it to the NBA. SEED is an acronym for Sports Education and Economic Development. It has most certainly lived up to its vision.

I got to see the Academy with my own eyes. The majority of the student-athletes there ranged from 6'5" to 7'1". I was like, *Gimme whatever they eating!* Between cities, we would drive sometimes up to ten to twelve hours on unpaved, bumpy roads. In some of the more remote areas we passed, I'd see people walking a mile or more to the nearest freshwater pump. So anytime we'd stop for a meal, I'd try to be extra mindful that I was privileged to be taken care of. At one home, we all sat on the floor while the family served us chicken that we ate with spoons. The very most delicious juice I had while there, and perhaps anywhere in the world, was green and called guitakh. I just didn't understand why it was so yummy.

When we did the clinic in Louga, a crowd of people hung out in the stands to watch as if it were a playoff game. Felt like us being there, foreigners giving back to the community by teaching b-ball skills at no charge to any participants, was something special and appreciated by all. The vibration was high-powered. After the drills, I passed out some of my NYC tournament gear and extra kicks I

Photo: Brian Benjamin

**01 73**

had in my bag to a few players to spread the love. As I walked out the park, two shoeless kids pointed at the Nikes I had on. I realized I hadn't seen a sneaker shop or sporting goods store the whole time we'd been there. So I took the high-tops off my feet and blessed one of the shorties with them, and received a priceless smile in return. Before I stepped foot into the van, the other preteen pointed at my socks. I didn't want to give him sweaty ones, so I went in my luggage and hit him off with a fresh pair. Then a group of youngins huddled around my window asking for some as well. I emptied out my supply for the trip.

When I told the story to die-hard sneaker heads back home, they thought I'd lost my noodle. There was a huge misconception about me, though. Because I was such a pivotal force in the culture as well as the footwear industry as an author, TV/radio personality, designer, customizer, consultant, ambassador, etc., people always thought I had hundreds of boxes in my closet. Press would constantly ask, "So . . . how many do you own, and what's your favorite?" I never considered myself a collector, though. I was a ballplayer first and foremost. So long as I had joints to ball in, I was straight. I didn't think nothing of letting go of what others perceived as valuable for resale or to sit on. On the low, I had been donating ten to twenty pairs of fresh-out-the-box or lightly worn kicks every few months ever since I found out about Hoops 4 Hope.

Because of my consistent advocacy and support, in 2010 Hoops 4 Hope honored me with their Ubuntu Award. *Ubuntu* translates to, *I am, because we are.* The other past recipients were coaches Larry Brown and "Doc" Rivers, winners of the 2004 and 2008 NBA Finals respectively, so I was in amazing company and completely humbled at the ceremony. During my acceptance speech, I mentioned that now I *had* to go visit the court in Harare, Zimbabwe,

Courtesy of Hoops 4 Hope

that they had dedicated in my name years prior. I didn't quite know how or when I was gonna get there, but the notion was put in the universe. I just had to embrace what was meant to happen . . .

Months later, I was invited to be the guest of honor at STR.CRD., Africa's first ever sneaker event. The producer booked me to speak on panels, sign books, play in a celebrity game to benefit Hoops 4 Hope, and DJ in Capetown and Johannesburg. *Ding ding ding!* Similar to my 2007 trip to Japan, I was engaging in my three passions, all in a foreign land. Lovely.

Except that land didn't feel so foreign to me.

In 2000, I had become the first US hip hop artist to ever perform in postapartheid South Africa. The visit was during the weekend of the sixth anniversary of the formation of the African National Congress. I did interviews on the top-rated TV talk show, *Phat Joe*, as well as the top radio station, YFM, to pump up the event, so the anticipation was bananas. I told the promoters I didn't want to stay in a hotel, rather in someone's crib so I could get a true sense of what their daily was like. As I walked out my host's apartment building to go to the venue, two kids ran up on me all excited, shouting, "Bobbito, Bobbito!" One grabbed my forearm and said, "Welcome home . . ." That sh*t sent chills up my spine.

I had protested against apartheid when I was a student at Wesleyan University where we'd have "Divest Now" rallies. I had seen how South African police would commit violence against peaceful protesters, some of whom were children advocating for human rights plus better schools and living conditions. Through Hugh Masekela's music, I learned about the exploitation of miners digging for gold who had a life expectancy of forty years due to the poor working environment. I took all this awareness with me on the trip, expecting to meet people who were emotionally scarred and bitter. So when I realized the strength and joy that every person I came across held in their heart, especially those living in the shantytowns where some homes were shacks with no running water, electricity, or proper sewage system, it was a testament to their life force and beyond.

In between the STR.CRD. events, I arranged a visit to the Hoops 4 Hope center in the Guguletha township, where I gave a clinic to the kids, partially in the rain. We all had so much ridiculous fun! That's when I decided I had to go to Harare once the sneaker activities were wrapped in South Africa. Zimbabwe was the next country over the border.

When I arrived at the Harare airport, the local newspaper sent photographers to capture the moment. My visit was a big deal to all involved. I was still pinching myself like, *Is this really happening?* As we drove up to the "Bobbito" court, my pulse rate increased, then my mind was blown. There were more than eighty kids there! The director of Hoops 4 Hope in Zimbabwe, Ngoni Mukukula, told me that players had shared that it was hard to hit long-range jumpers there. So the first drill I went through with the group was jump-shot form. There weren't enough balls to go around, so I just had them hold an imaginary one. We worked on crossovers, passing, etc. I could have stayed there the rest of the day and night, then literally slept on the asphalt.

Over the decades, I'd had a recurring dream where I was playing ball at an outdoor dirt court in Africa, surrounded by gorgeous trees on a rich green field. I'd jump from half-court, then glide until I caught a butter roll at the rim. Sometimes I'd catch a two-hand dunk. These serene moments in my sleep mostly occurred prior to Hoops 4 Hope dedicating a

Courtesy of Hoops 4 Hope

court in my name, then came here and there leading up to my Harare visit. I reflected the future in the subconsciousness of my past.

Indeed, I felt home.

Hoops 4 Hope had five centers throughout the Harare area. I went to each and gave clinics, did tricks, danced along with the kids to their songs, and simply absorbed the wonderful energy each of the youthful groups gave me. I was in absolute awe of them. At one of the courts, I was greeted with a handwritten *Welcome Bobbito* sign that melted my heart. A young girl handed me a letter. Later that evening, I read it:

**REFLECTION ETERNAL**

My name is CONFIDENTIAL I am a girl age 11. I am light in Complexion. I am the only child in my family. I lost my parents when I was two years old. They both died of H.I.V. and I am also positive. I had noone to take care of me nobody likes me because of my status. Thank you Bobito for giving me shoes. I never knew that in my life I would wear sneakers.

Thanks

Babito

May god bless

I could never again complain about getting my sneakers dirty, not having the latest exclusive pair, or any of that sh*t. I lived a very privileged life in my heyday of doing events and designing for various brands and getting hit off with product for free. I had been a key face of the culture, but experiencing what Hoops 4 Hopes was doing on the ground in Africa just made me feel like the bottom of my shoes had given out on me. All the props and recognition felt meaningless.

At the next clinic, I noticed that one of the coaches had a hot pair of kicks on. Then I realized . . . they used to be mine. I had donated them years prior. Ever since that day, whenever the press asks me the mundane question, "So . . . what are your favorite sneakers?" I respond with, "The ones I've donated."

I reflect you because we reflect each other.

# The Park is my Church

Photo: Justin Francis

My experiences in Senegal, South Africa, and Zimbabwe were not just life-defining, but life-affirming. I gained a stronger sense of purpose in all that I had been doing for so many years to grow the game. What struck me, though, was that similar to my contributions to hip hop, I had to be very active *in person*. For me to affect lives using basketball as a tool for social change, I needed to create a beacon that could shine light in a passive manner, one that didn't require me traveling all over the world every weekend, as much as I would've loved to. So . . .

I decided to write/direct/produce/narrate/music supervise my first film—with zero knowledge of how to really make one.

In 2004, a young b-ball junkie named Kevin Couliau based in France had mailed a photo of his friend dunking on their local playground to me, and I ran it in an early issue of *Bounce Magazine*. Kev had never been published before, so that became the launch of his photography career. He continued contributing to *Bounce* while I was editor in chief, and did the same for *Reverse* in France. In 2009, he added videography to his artistic palette, and directed a music video titled "Heart and Soul of New York City." I was overseas when I first watched it, and was moved by his ability to capture nuance. I felt like I was back home, and put the piece on repeat ten times in a row. Because he wasn't from NY, his lens was on courts within the architecture of a greater urban landscape. Where someone saw a rim and a backboard, Kev saw project buildings and pigeons in the background and included them in frame. Really striking work.

So I hit him up: "What are you doing next summer?" He replied, "I'm currently collecting unemployment insurance from the French government and looking for work." Perfect. I was single with no kids, no roommates, nothing. I told him, "Come sleep on my couch for a few months and let's make a documentary . . ."

Kevin's backpack was stuffed with his camera and audio equipment. Mine had my ball, talent/location release forms, permits, notes, list of questions, schedule, maps, yadda yadda. Together we visited 180 courts throughout all five boroughs in seventy-five days, 99 percent of them on our bicycles. We interviewed legends and park regulars just the same. Didn't matter if they were men, women, teenagers, elderly, whatever. If they had a passionate story about playing pickup outdoors, we hit record. My boy Turk was a warden at Rikers Island, and somehow arranged for us to come film the inmates there.

Rikers Island photo: Jon Lopez

0181

One night I stumbled onto a run at Crack Is Wack Park where all the players used sign language to communicate. I respectfully asked if we could capture their world, and was welcomed with open arms. I was surpassing my vision for the film to be inclusive and a true representation of the city's diversity, by far.

I came out of pocket to fund everything, not knowing if I'd ever break even or make any money back. I knew we were on to something, though. Amazingly, there had never been a documentary made about pickup basketball in New York. The Mecca. How could that be? Every ballplayer this city has ever produced started out in the park. I had to make this project happen. I had faith in the vision.

Aside from filming, at 100 percent of the stops, Kevin and I played. I never made all-city anything, but no matter where we went—Bronx, Manhattan, Brooklyn, Queens, Staten Island—players recognized me and showed love. Perhaps my favorite day of shooting was when we hit Jefferson Park in East Harlem. As thousands of cars drove by on FDR Drive, there was a five-on-five with Mexican players making calls in Spanish on one side, and preteens and teenagers playing 21, Knock-Out, 50, and Sign-Out on the other.

In the 1970s and 1980s, Jefferson was simply called "The Court," attracting the top talent from national powerhouse Ben Franklin HS just steps away. The school's 1978 leading scorer and rebounder, Billy Rieser, grew up on that block and earned the nickname "White Jesus" for getting funky above the rim. The 6'4" guard with a forty-four-inch vertical was unique in that he only wanted to dunk so long as it was *on someone's head*. If the highflier had a clear lane or breakaway, he'd just lay the ball up. "Jumping Billy" is one of the most legendary dunkers Harlem has ever produced in any era, regardless of background. My childhood buddy Lincoln Parker once told me, "Billy had the most insane hops for a whiteboy I've ever seen!"

Although I was cognizant of Rieser's history as I walked into Jefferson, the teenagers balling out there that day were clueless. One kid was hawkin' me hard with his mouth open, and I wasn't really sure why, until . . .

"Excuse me, mister, but . . . aren't you Bobbito García?"

I nodded my head.

"See, I told you!" the diesel sixteen-year-old screamed out to his boys. "That's the dude from *NBA Streets*! My name's Nugget. Wanna play one-on-one?"

I smiled and jokingly asked, "You sure?" as I walked onto the court. Confidence will throw an opponent off before you even check up. I told him, "Okay, then, guard up . . ."

The kid could play! The game was close, until I did a 360 spin with my right pivot foot planted, jabbed left, went hard back to my right, dribbled forward, then *boop*, stepped back mean. The kid bit every move hard, and on the last one, he found his back foot sliding as he lost his balance and put his hands to the ground to break his fall. His friends all screamed in unison, "Oh!" as they ran off the bench onto the court. They all taunted him repeatedly, "He cut you!"

The kid was embarrassed, and now I had the mental advantage.

At point, I finished him with a simple jab step, cross through, hard layup to the right. I immediately told the kid, "Good game," and extended my hand to give him a pound and a hug. As I walked away, my earnest challenger looked me dead in my eye and shared, "It was a for-real honor to play with you." He only knew me as a public figure, had no idea what I'd been through in my life to get to the point to hear that from a stranger. "That means a lot, my brother. Thank *you*." I felt emotional afterward.

The kid made my day.

When *Doin' It in the Park: Pick-Up Basketball, NYC* premiered at the 2012 Urbanworld Film Festival, mine and Kevin's baby won the Audience Award for Best Feature. Nike caught wind and put us on a tour through eleven international cities where we screened the documentary, did Q&As afterward, and of course found the local run to play ball. I didn't just rely on the big dogs to raise awareness. I went straight grassroots and reached out to club promoters, basketball organizers, and whoever else worldwide to produce one-time events. By the time PBS and Netflix picked up the broadcast rights, I had personally booked over a hundred screenings throughout six continents.

What had started out as a small idea in my head that I then shared with Kev to help me put on film became a motivational force globally, galvanizing players of all backgrounds to get out to their local park. The film's impact ultimately put the battery in my backpack for my next project . . .

Photo: Joel Koukoui

Photographer unknown

Photo: Trigger Images HK

Photo: Juan Cruz

The game 21 had always been one of my favorite cultural aspects of NYC's pickup world, so naturally I wrote a scene about it for *Doin' It in the Park*. And no matter who we interviewed, as soon as I asked the question about their experiences playing with no teammates/every-one-for-themselves, a light would shine brightly in their eye as they reminisced. At one of our postscreening Q&As, Kevin explained that in his hometown of Nantes, France, if they didn't have enough for a three-on-three, they just went home. And the light bulb went off in my head. What if I could create basketball's first ever 21 tournament, and provide a new context for players worldwide to engage with the sport?

In 2013, mi hermano Boricua Manny Maldonado had a lunchtime run at the Boys' Club in East Harlem. He announced, "We playing 21 to warm up . . . full court . . ." My mind was blown. Not half-court like I had experienced my whole life, but full court? Everyone defended whoever had the ball. On a change of possession, the action went the opposite way, just like a normal five-on-five. The first time I touched the rock, I got triple-teamed, and that was *ninety feet away* from the rim. I absolutely loved the challenge. Each time I scored, I thought, *Sh\*t, if I can get a bucket on nine defenders, how is anyone gonna guard me one-on-one?* The confidence I built that afternoon, along with the grueling physical demands on my lungs from constantly sprinting back and forth, was ridiculous. The fun I had was supremely unmatched compared to any other context I'd ever experienced in the sport. Sold.

In the summer of 2013, I debuted my tournament, Full Court 21, at 77th Street and Riverside Park. My vision was inclusivity. Sure, I invited playground legends like Headache, Jack Ryan, and Speedy, but local HS kids who loved the game, park regulars, and recreational weekend warriors of all ages and backgrounds were welcomed as well. In the very first game, I had two women suit up right alongside the men. My homeboy from Chinatown who had never balled uptown laced up, too. Midseason, three players in town visiting from Amsterdam signed up the day of. They had hit me up wanting to experience the Rucker and West 4th, but I told them, "Unless you're 6'9" or above, you can't just roll up and expect to get a uniform at either. And there's no tryouts." So they were extra appreciative of my open format to experience authentic NYC b-ball culture against great comp while I was on the mic talkin' sh\*t and giving out nicknames.

Expansion happened organically, and in the following years FC21 was produced in more than thirty-five cities throughout five continents, including my homeland of Puerto Rico as well as Havana, Cuba, where I'd never been prior but had always dreamed of visiting. In Paris, a record two hundred–plus registrants competed for the chance to advance to the All-World Final. That whole afternoon, countless men and women came up to me to express gratitude because they loved basketball but had never participated in a tournament. They played outside of the local club or university circuit. My concept allowed them to feel part of a global movement. I was hitting my goal of inclusivity with a bullseye.

Then, in 2016, I moved the NYC qualifiers to the Goat aka Rock Steady, the park that raised me. Not only was I producing the tournament, I was also announcing, then putting the mic down and jumping into games myself—at the tender age of fifty. I couldn't have been any happier. Everything was coming together, and every summer the number of participants grew and grew.

The 2019 FC21 All-World Final was the most celebrated night in the history of the tournament. NBA stars Baron Davis and Lance Stephenson as well as Harlem Globetrotter "Mani Love" all showed up to watch. The park was packed like it was the 1970s all over again and Earl Manigault was reigning supreme over all competition. Was an honor for me to continue his legacy of attracting great talent to 99th Street for the community to enjoy spectating for free.

Photo: Imani Vidal

Italian national team member Martina Fassina grabbed the women's crown that evening, edging out "Nutso" from Japan as well as the best field of FC21 ladies I had ever assembled, with Berlin, Barcelona, Paris, and NYC all represented. The men's final was a battle as well. Award-winning author/journalist Jesse Washington got the crowd amped when he dribbled between his defender's legs, hit the eighteen-footer, then glanced at Lance Stephenson on the sideline and mimicked his air-guitar dance. While that highlight went viral, Demitri Harris aka "Demi Sosa" was putting on the most entertaining single-game performance in my tournament's history, amassing the highest total blocks and dunks before hitting the game-winning tiebreaker shot against the 2013 and 2016 champion Matt Thomas aka "Viva Las Vegas!" from Harlem. Even though the hometown hero lost, heads were showing ridiculous love to Demi, who had flown in all the way from Vancouver.

I closed the night out on the mic by proudly saying, "Much love to everyone here for being part of the first and only one-on-five basketball tournament in the world. We'll see you next year, peeeace!" As the park emptied out, I sat in my portable chair, feeling both exhausted and accomplished. Two thousand ballplayers worldwide participated in FC21 that summer. By 2019, more than 100,000 viewers had enjoyed me and Kevin's film. Both had started out as light bulbs in my head, but now had their own legs. A decade prior, I'd envisioned creating platforms that could motivate and inspire people of all ages and backgrounds that did not require my physical presence to function, and I carried out that mission to a T, man.

In my mind, basketball was a religion, the park was my church, and in this scenario I led the faithful as a righteous man of the cloth would, except instead of a cleric's collar, I was rockin' baggy b-ball shorts and high-tops.

Opposite page photos: David "Dee" Delgado

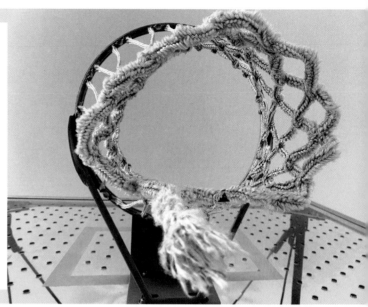

# THE BOX THAT ROCKS

In 2019, the only tournament I was playing in was . . . my own. I was neither coaching any squads nor training individuals anymore. Nike hadn't booked me to announce any games since 2015. My annual Elite 24 gig had come to a halt in 2014. My career as a freestyle performer doing halftime shows at big arenas had run its course, too. I barely had time to play pickup, even though I was in the playground daily. My life was drastically different because I had a new responsibility—doing my part to raise a child. My co-parent was dealing with some health issues, so I had become the full-time primary caretaker of our son. I couldn't be at the court focused on how to beat my man off the hezi so I could get to the cup for a two-piece. No. I watched our little one at the park caringly and diligently, making sure he wasn't wandering off, getting into a fight, or scraping his flesh after taking a spill. I'd keep my eye on him while doing stationary dribbling drills and jump shots into the air from the bench. If there were kids playing *21* on the other side of the fence, I'd glance over with a burning desire to jump in, but I'd stay my course. Family first.

Selfishly, I needed FC21 badly. My tournament was the only consistent b-ball activity in my life at that point that deeply connected me to my NY roots. The fact that by 2019 I was no longer coming out of pocket to fund the qualifiers and was finally getting support from sponsors made producing it even sweeter. Being able to provide for my family and community using a round ball that only weighed twenty-two ounces was just brilliant, and, as had been the case my entire life, completely unexpected.

Almost equally unanticipated was the day my lil' shorty, right before his sixth birthday and on his own will, asked if he could learn how to play ball. While he was acutely aware of how much I loved the game, and had witnessed me announcing FC21, I never pushed the sport on him. Of course I fantasized about the two of us sharing the passion, but I didn't need to raise a mini-me or have people calling him "Lil' Bobbito." I wanted our child to be his own person.

In the winter of '19–'20, shorty rock and I starting shooting around together whenever he showed interest. Our family had moved to Crown Heights, Brooklyn, so we had multiple courts within a hop-skip to choose from, including Brower, St. John's, 316, Lincoln Terrace, Jackie Robinson, and St. Andrew's on Kingston which had the biddy rims. Dunking on eight-foot baskets brought me back to my own childhood getting bizzy at PS 84. The low height was great for my goofy six-year-old neophyte, too. I attempted to teach him proper jump-shot form while saying, "Don't forget the goose neck," to make him laugh, but he much preferred old-school underhanded scoopers à la Hall of Famer Calvin Murphy—with his eyes closed and back to the basket. Oh boy.

Our asphalt giggle fests were a sweet balance of learning and fun. My son didn't need a drill sergeant trying to prepare him for the NBA at age six. I once trained a young girl who had serious potential. During our first session, her father kept screaming at her from the sidelines to do better. She slipped and fell during one of the drills, and I heard, "You're not hurt, get up!" as I helped her back to her feet. I walked over and respectfully explained that I understood he was trying to encourage her, and perhaps toughen her skin, but that I'd prefer he left the area, or at least stayed quiet. From that point on, the future college player blossomed under my guidance. The constant pressure from her dad had been debilitating. I certainly wasn't ever going to stress my own kid out by pushing him to be the player I was, or surpass the levels I achieved.

My co-parent suggested we try the method of self-directed learning at our home where we would trust our child's natural curiosity and facilitate whatever interests he had. I bought into the concept wholeheartedly, as my parents had given me a lot of educational independence as well. So long as our kid was expanding his horizons in a safe and healthy manner, I knew he'd be straight. My dream of showing up to the Goat with my son and calling, "Next!" held no weight compared to us giving him the tools to have a productive and positive mindset toward life, on his own terms.

As 2020 kicked in, I needed to grasp onto all the positivity within my reach. That first month, Kobe Bryant died in a helicopter crash. I had interviewed the five-time NBA champion for *Vibe* and ESPN, plus at two Nike events, and was always impressed that he remembered my name when we'd bump heads. Didn't hurt that the b-ball savant knew we both played for the same high school. Although we were never close, his death was still felt. The "Black Mamba" was one of the greatest players ever. I was one of millions who was inspired by his laser focus to be the best he could possibly be. What stung me in particular about the news was that his thirteen-year-old daughter Gianna was a victim of the tragedy as well. I had to block out the thought of being in an accident with my own child while knowing that neither of us would come out of the descent alive. Yeesh. So . . .

I went to Brower Park K-Solo and put up jumpers with my opposite hand for an hour to honor the ambidextrous midrange shooter Kobe Bryant was. My favorite moment interviewing him was when we both admitted that we used to brush our teeth with our left hand to help strengthen our weak side. Then I added that even as an adult I still did toe raises while brushing, and he was like, "You too?!" Was a hilarious reveal and indicative of how it didn't matter if you retired as the third-leading scorer in NBA history or were a dedicated ballplayer for life, the love for the game and the ways to improve could be shared by all. I thought about our exchange as I played one-on-one outside that afternoon, left hand vs. right hand. Every time my left scored, I yelled out, "Kobe!"

I got booked to DJ in Paris on March 6, 2020. My co-parent, who is also a best friend who sincerely cares about my well-being, advised me not to go. She had been following news overseas about a novel coronavirus, and was concerned about me catching it while traveling. In all my years of gigs, I had only ever canceled on a promoter once, though, and that was because I was in the emergency room dealing with kidney stones on the day of the outgoing flight. Otherwise, I always kept my word. Business reasons aside, I loved my global community of friends and supporters, and didn't want to disappoint those anticipating my performance. I had deep relationships in the City of Love, too, as I spent months there while editing/producing *Doin' It in the Park*. So I decided to go.

A lot changed quickly over that weekend. I got back to New York on Monday the eighth, and by Thursday the eleventh, the NBA announced that the season was suspended indefinitely due to the international spread of SARS-CoV-2, which was not only making people incredibly sick, but was claiming lives left and right at a rapid pace. I had only ever seen league action stop due to player union disputes.

I felt fortunate for having returned from Paris safely, but also hardheaded for not having listened to my co-parent's advice. I had put her, our child, and myself all at risk. I didn't want to be responsible for bringing sickness, or worse death, into our home. I had to be more thoughtful. So moving forward I gave more credence to her insights, did my own research, and ultimately trusted her guidance on how to best protect our family.

The following weeks, shelter-in-place orders started to take effect in certain parts of the US. New York City became the epicenter of the pandemic, accounting for the highest spread in the world. In particular, our neighborhood was being hit stupid hard. The nursing home down the block from the crib unfortunately turned into a makeshift morgue. I heard over fifty elderly people died there. My uncle was living in a senior care facility, too, but in the BX. His son called me to share that mi tío had passed, and explained that his father, who was otherwise in decent physical health, had been experiencing problems breathing the last time they spoke on the phone. I didn't even ask what the cause of death was. Didn't need to.

On March 17, a dear cousin of mine died of cancer. Her loss weighed heavy on my heart, especially knowing that I wouldn't be able to support her family and attend the services. Her husband, who I loved equally, met her when they were teenagers, and they'd lived in the same apartment for fifty years. He committed suicide two months later. I imagined that being alone in grief during the period of shelter-in-place didn't help his situation.

The media coverage of the pandemic felt dystopian. The personal losses were chipping away at my spirit. And the pandemic's unknowns were daunting. The masses didn't know how they were getting COVID. Was the virus passed by touching surfaces? Was it aerial? Both? I needed air. I needed a ball in my hand. I needed an outdoor court to shoot jumpers on. Sh*t was getting to be too much.

As a measure to mitigate the spread, the NYC Department of Education shut down public schools on March 16, and our son was switched to remote learning from home, which was honestly a relief. Instead of being in a crowded classroom with thirty students, he'd be safe with us. When I'd take him to the park, we'd mask up, stay off the high-touch areas of the playground equipment, and shoot around by ourselves to ensure social distancing. Was crazy that my favorite thing to do became the safest activity we could engage in as well.

The Zoom classes were stressing my kid out from jump, so I started using the court as our outdoor classroom. I told him dribbles were worth a nickel, layups a dime, and backward shots with his eyes closed a quarter. I'd let him play while tallying all the values in his head. If he came out with the wrong total, we'd work together to figure out why. Then I would shoot fifteen-footers and threes, and he was tasked with keeping track of my makes and misses. He'd share, "Eight went in, and two were off." And I'd come back with, "Cool! What was the ratio?" He'd reply, "8:10, Papá." Finally, I'd say, "Okay, now convert that into a percentage," and he'd proudly answer, "Eighty percent!"

I always thought a basketball court could be a fertile learning environment. Teaching my child math at my personal house of prayer was pure joy, and the very best therapy for me to deal with the early days of the pandemic. I wasn't alone in using b-ball as a therapeutic method. Even though the city was recommending that people stay home or social distance when they were outside, heads in Crown Heights were still on the asphalt balling. And I'm not talking about shooting by themselves as I was doing. Nah. Cats were playing Utah, three-on-three, etc., and guarding up closely, Brooklyn hard work steez. I wondered if this was their way to escape the drama of how COVID-19 was affecting us all, or if they were numb to the news announcements due to lack of trust or access. Or . . . maybe it was indicative of how some people of color in the hood don't expect to survive past their teens anyhow due to gun violence, gangs, incarceration, lack of access to proper housing, healthy food, and education, as well as other conditions that plague their future . . . so why not ball out as if it was your last day on earth?

I understood.

Whatever the cause, NYC had to reduce the out-of-control spread, whether individuals were being mindful of others or not. On March 24, I noticed a big yellow sign hung with zip ties on the fence by the entrance to St. Andrew's:

Heads continued to play. Basketball has always been an unstoppable force in this city. What occurred next was something I never thought I'd see in my whole entire existence: the NYC Department of Parks & Recreation took the rims down. In every park. Citywide.

The first naked backboard I saw at St. Andrew's made me feel like Parks & Rec had grabbed the heart out my chest, stomped it on the ground, then pointed at my sad face while laughing. I couldn't believe my eyes. I went to Brower. *Nada.* I checked St. John's, where there's six full courts. No outdoor rims anywhere. In the mecca of the sport? Was I experiencing a horror movie come to life? What the f, man? My son and I were using them safely while distancing, and the daily activity was my life support. I *needed* that reprieve. Even so, for the benefit of community health, it was the right thing to do. Sucked, but if it meant mitigating disease and ultimately saving lives, then I was with it.

Days later, a friend who lived nearby and knew I was fiendin' to play let me know she saw some kids shooting around at night in the schoolyard on Sterling off Albany Avenue. Apparently someone had cut a hole in the fence so that they could access the court. My heart started racing in anticipation. The very next afternoon, I tried walking over, but I was too amped up and started running there. I turned the corner off Albany, and indeed, the rims were still up. But as I got closer, I noticed the fence had already been patched up. Fuuuh . . .

Stepping back on the court felt like returning to a fatal crime scene too soon, so I took some weeks off to reconfigure my balance. I picked up my weighted jump rope for the first time in over a decade. Jumping pregame to loosen up had been mandatory for my routine, until I injured my shoulder. I wasn't rusty at all, though, and immediately caught my rhythm executing the crisscross, high knee, double under, and side under with decent footwork. I also started running the stairs in my building, first to pick up the mail, then eventually increasing the trips until I'd gone up and down six flights at least five times in a row.

My workouts were contributing to a new sense of self. I went 100 percent plant-based, and even fasted for three days for the first time in my life to support a friend who was observing Ramadan. To minimize risks, I stopped doing gigs that required in-person appearances, which meant I wasn't traveling—at all. I did not miss dealing with jet lag, either. I was able to create a consistent eating schedule for the first time in my adult life. Gone were the late-night snacks after coming home from a club at four a.m., as well as the sh*tty airport terminal food to avoid even sh*ttier in-flight meals in god knows what time zone. Within a month, I dropped fifteen pounds and hit my high school playing weight of 155 for the first time in thirty-six years. I had no intention of shedding; it just happened, and my body thanked me. I started sleeping better. I felt rested.

A friend noticed my glow and tried to tell me the pandemic had a "silver lining." I stopped him before he could even finish his sentence. I said: "Nah, b. Hundreds of thousands of people are dying. There is no 'silver lining' to that. Please don't say that . . ."

I was particularly sensitive. COVID-19 claimed the lives of nine friends and family members that first year of the pandemic. I also saw the effects up close and personal as my co-parent got sick. Because she was immunocompromised and chronically ill to begin with, the virus hit her hard. She dealt with the blow, started feeling better, then got smacked with a second round. Thirty-five days after quarantining in her bedroom, she rejoined me and our son in our household. And to this day, she suffers from long COVID symptoms, including damage to her neurological, cardiac, and circulatory systems. So no, for me there was no silver lining. At all.

Jumping rope, running stairs, eating well, and feeling rested were all prepping me for where I really wanted to be—back on the asphalt. I felt rejuvenated and so thankful to be healthy. I started hitting Brower with my kid again on the regular, taking my heavy ball as well as my regular one, doing ballhandling drills to get my sweat on while shorty played with his Frisbee or whatever other outdoor toy. We had two full courts all to ourselves. No one else was out there.

Then one day, I said, *F this sh\*t. Nothing and no one can stop me from enjoying this game. Not my college coach, not the weather, and not the pandemic.* So I started shooting . . . on the backboard . . . with no rim . . . *using the taped-up box in the middle as my target.* And I felt liberated. Jab step, spin, pump fake, pound dribble, step back, shot . . . Over and over again. I was straight going hard doing jump-shot drills, not moving to the next spot until I hit ten from each.

Gino, the OG on the block who had played high-level ball in the seventies, stopped me on the sidewalk the next day to say, "Yo, man, you had me f\*cked up yesterday . . ." I didn't know where he was going with this, but I respectfully listened. "I can see the court from my apartment window, and when I saw you out there yesterday shooting, I got so amped I put my sneakers on and raced down to join you. But when I got closer, I realized the rims still weren't up. You were going so hard, I literally thought they *had* to be back finally. Dag . . ."

I identified with Gino's disappointment deeply and wanted to give him a pound and a hug, but even in moments of knee-jerk reactions to others' emotions, I had to check myself and maintain social distancing. I told my neighbor, "The rims will be back up soon, my brother. I know they will." I gave Gino a nod and kept it moving.

Months passed, and I continued to use the box on the backboard as my target. I thought, *When they put the rims back up, my bank shot is gonna be fiyah.* I had to keep finding positives out of the bizarreness that was our daily reality. I received an email from Parks & Rec that they weren't giving out permits for the summer of 2020, so there went my dream of elevating FC21 after our banner year. With no rims up in June, I kind of expected that the tournament wasn't gonna happen anyhow.

On the first day of July, my b-ball buddy for life Jesse Washington reached out with some good news: "Bob, don't quote me on this, but my cousin works for Parks & Rec so I got the inside scoop. The rims are going back up soon, bro. Looks like Brooklyn is scheduled for July 6." Wooord. I didn't allow myself to get too pumped up for fear of getting disappointed again like the time I went to Sterling off Albany, but his words were like seeing your parents hiding a box in the closet days before your birthday, knowing it's for you. The disclosure was a welcome tease.

I put the thought out my head for the weekend, and then the sixth rolled up. The sun was beaming by noon so I had started taking my boy out in the mornings. Since we lived in Crown Heights, I figured Parks & Rec wouldn't get that deep into BK until the afternoon, but it was still comforting to hope that by the following day, there was a great chance the rims would be back up. I felt antsy. And then . . .

At eleven a.m., a Parks & Rec truck rolled up onto the court at Brower. Felt like the world stopped around me, and things were moving in slow motion. I didn't even rebound my jump shot. The ball dribbled itself out of bounds. Two workers got out and proceeded to open the vehicle's cargo bed, taking out a toolbox, a ladder, and . . . a rim. A rim! My son could sense my excitement, so he stood next to me at half-court as we both watched in awe. I had gone four months without shooting on a precious orange-painted metal goal, the longest stretch in forty years. My heart was tingling, and the muscles in my hands, arms, and shoulders actually tensed up. Since March, I had only practiced on the box of the backboard. What was it going to feel like to put up a jumper on an official basket again?

The workers tightened the last nut and bolt, looked at us, then said, "We're done. It's all yours." The rim looked like a halo. It had never appeared so radiant to me prior. I grabbed my rock and stepped up, but then I paused, having nothing to do with the beautiful butterflies that just materialized in my stomach.

I handed the ball to my son instead, then said, "Go 'head. You take the first shot." He got in his underhand scooper position, and launched a doozy that was high enough but fell a few feet short. I encouraged him by saying, "Good try!" Then, on his second attempt, the pill took one bounce on the back of the goal and SPLASH. "Alright, kid!" A few people had gathered on the side to watch and were clapping for him, too. What an unforgettable experience to share with my youngin.

As the workers moved to the next backboard, I picked up the rock and daringly stepped out to the three-point line. F it.

*Let's jump in where we left off!* pivot foot declared. I talked myself through the poetry in motion: *Step in. Square to the basket in the triple-threat position. Lift the arm and jump in one motion, then release with rotation. Guide hand perpendicular to my face, and leave the goose neck up to let the defender see the flavor . . .*

*Wahkah.* I rebounded the ball, and dribbled back to the three-point line behind the top of the key. *Wahkah* again. I thought, *Nothing shakin' but the turkey bacon,* and shot another trey whop. Not a morsel of metal was touched; we talking strictly net particles swimming in the breeze. Swisharoni sauce three times to the fullest.

I stopped there cuz the temperature was rising and I had to get shorty-rock back to the crib for cool air and vittles. Before we dipped out, I recorded a video to post on social. In one take, I went off the top of my head and spoke freely: "Ayo! I feel like I just climaxed, yo. I feel like I just saw the most high supreme being appear in my local court. THE RIMS ARE BACK UP, YO, WORD UP!!!"

I walked up to the Parks & Rec workers to share gratitude: "I don't think I can express to you how much joy you brought to me and my son today, so thank you."

One responded by saying, "Man, at every park we've been to today, people have been clapping for us when we leave."

I told him, "I don't doubt that, and well deserved. Can I . . . offer you a tip?" I had a twenty-spot in my pocket ready but would have happily given him a Ben Franklin.

The humble man then explained, "Very kind of you, but as city employees, we can't accept gratuities for our services."

So I ended with: "Ah, okay. Gotchu. Well, just know that what you did just now for our park uplifted my soul. *My soul.* So from the bottom of my heart, thank you. Thank you!"

Janet Jackson's lyric, "*You don't know what you got till it's gone,*" popped in my head. I had forever looked at an outdoor court as an open space for all to enjoy no matter their background, but I had taken for granted that even that hallowed ground could be taken away. The pandemic's shelter-in-place and rim removals were measures that restricted access. Stepping forward, I had to fully recognize the supreme privilege of being able to shoot jumpers on the asphalt. I could *never* look at playing ball the same again. I didn't think this was possible, but with a newfound appreciation of the game, I fell in love with it even deeper than I'd ever imagined.

I am mystified by how meaningful basketball has become in my life.

# EPILOGUE

A year into the pandemic, a documentary went into production about the most impactful point guards out of New York during the eighties and nineties, focusing on the narratives of Kenny Anderson, Pearl Washington, Rod Strickland, Shammgod, Rafer Alston, Stephon Marbury, Kenny Smith, and Mark Jackson. One of the producers, Chad Gittens, who was also a b-ball buddy, reached out to me about being interviewed so that I could break down the history, folklore, and nuances of each of these legends, saying, "We can't make this film without your voice, Bob. We *need* you on camera for this." NBA superstar Kevin Durant and Showtime were the backers, so this project screamed success.

I was honored and humbled, though I explained to him that I wasn't doing any in-person appearances: "My co-parent is immunocompromised and chronically ill, fam. I'm her full-time caregiver as well as the primary caretaker of our son while homeschooling him. I'm masked up and distancing, even outside, to minimize risks best possible. I hope you understand . . ."

Chad heard me loud and clear. He promised me a film set outdoors where the cinematographer, lighting technician, and sound engineer on down would be masked up, PCR tested, and distanced, with no exceptions, plus there'd be a safety director on-site to ensure everyone was following strict protocol the entire time. I had heard how seriously the movie industry was approaching mitigation during the pandemic, so that made me comfortable and I decided to go on camera.

Photo: Chad Gittens

Even though Chad's crew was small, I caught an adrenaline rush like I was in front of an audience again. The director, Sam Eliad, started asking me questions, and I went into a zone. I answered as if I were performing in front of five thousand people, animated, moving, gesturing, and laughing while lovingly sharing stories of watching Pac Man, Skip to My Lou, Shammgod, etc., work miracles on the asphalt. I was on such a b-ball high that when they wrapped me, I hit 258 in Bed-Stuy to shoot jumpers until the sun went down. I literally woke up the next morning still thinking about what I had said in the interview. Felt truly inspired, and grateful to have contributed.

With the amount of huge NBA names they were interviewing as well, I was thinking they'd keep two or three of my best anecdotes, and the rest of what I shared would wind up on the editing-room floor. Then in 2022, I got a call from Dao-Yi Chow, who had attended the star-studded red-carpet premiere of Showtime's *NYC Point Gods*, and my former mentee said, "Bob, I didn't know you narrated this film. It's so f*ckin' dope!"

Photo: Chad Gittens

And I was like, "Nah, you buggin'. I was just a regular-schmegular interviewee in that."

Then D responded, "Nah, b. *You* buggin'. You in damn near every scene, and got more screen time than Steven A. Smith!"

"Whaaa?!!!"

I waited patiently for the broadcast premiere, and lo and behold, Dao-Yeezy wasn't gassin' me. Not only was my hairline all up in mad scenes yapping away throughout acts one, two, and three, but the "Characteristic of a NYC Point God: Handles" section opened up with b-roll footage of . . . me dribbling my ball while freestyling in Harlem. Mind blown, kapow!

When *NYC Point Gods* was nominated in the forty-fourth annual Sports Emmy Awards's Outstanding Long Documentary category, I reached out to Chad to congratulate him. My dude hit me right back with a jewel: "*We* did that, b! You a big part of that. Sam and our whole crew had an incredible film, but when we got you on camera, your interview solidified everything and took the narrative to another level. So thank you."

Perhaps the illest component of being involved for me was seeing how Chad and director Sam Eliad identified me in *NYC Point Gods*. On the bottom of the screen when I first appear on camera, the lower-third graphic reads: *Bobbito García, B-ball Sage*. I started as a scrub in my early years, then after decades of ridiculous dedication to the game, I have earned the title "sage" as I approach my sixties. Not bad for a Puerto Rican kid from the Goat who not a soul would have predicted would make an entire career out of loving basketball with global impact, whether storytelling, documenting, curating, teaching, announcing, performing, playing, advocating, or simply inspiring others by example.

On October 17, 2023, Chad Gittens passed away. To honor him, I grabbed my ball and headed to my local outdoor court, then shot jumpers for an hour while putting positive thoughts in my head about the brother. I wonder if dribbling is to me what the sound of drums was to my ancestors. The vibration in both cases elicits a transcendent path to an alternate reality, one that to me feels celestial and safe.

I'll keep dribbling. Bong bong!

Lettering: José Parlá

# THE PARK PICKUP PLAYER

I AM NOT THE NBA OR EURO LEAGUE
I DON'T EARN STACKS OR SIGN CONTRACTS
I AM NOT HIGH SCHOOL OR COLLEGE
I AM FOREVER ELIGIBLE
I HAVE NO AGENT
I MAKE TEMPORARY VERBAL AGREEMENTS LIKE:
"YEAH. I'LL RUN WITH YOU"
"WHAT'S THE SQUAD?"
"HIT OR MISS"
"OUR ROCK"
"GAME'S SIXTEEN BY ONES"
"WIN BY TWO, 21 STRAIGHT"
"FENCE IS OUT"
"THIS BALL SUCKS!"
THERE ARE NO ZEBRAS IN THIS ZOO
AND NO GOVERNMENT CHEESE LINE

Lettering: LEE Quiñones, José Parlá

I CALL, "MY BALL,"
TAKE IT OUT AND DO IT TO 'EM AGAIN
I DON'T JUST PENETRATE DOWN THE LANE
I TAKE IT DOWN DEATH VALLEY
TO THE SAUCE PAN, THE WELL
TO THE BAJA
I DON'T JUST CROSSOVER
I PUT YOU IN THE SPIN CYCLE AND RINSE
I GETS LIGHT

I DISCO, BOOGIE, AND SKATE ON MY MAN
I GOT THE WIGGLES, THE BOP-BOP, THE WHIP-WHOP
THE LEGAL YO-YO
DON'T REACH UNLESS YOU WANNA GET BUGGED
I WILL CRACK YOU, FOOLISH

Lettering: BlusterOne © Alice Mizrachi

I DONT JUST STEAL THE BALL
I FORCE TURNOVERS WHERE YOU HAVE NO HANDLE
PICK THE POCKETS AND YELL,
"POKED"! BOOP"!

GIMME DAT
I DONT JUST SCORE
I GETS BUCKETS
I WANNA COOK AND EMBARRASS
YOU AND YOUR WHOLE SQUAD

HEZI. STEP BACK. RATTY FOR THE TREY-VOP
ICE WATER, BANG BANG—
HAH, AND-ONE, HOLD THAT
— GAME —
IF I SO HAPPEN TO TAKE AN L, I NEGOTIATE
"RUN IT!"          "YOU GOT YOUR
                    FIVE?"
"WHO GOT NEXT?"

Lettering: Fernando Ruiz Lorenzo (ETERNAL), CHINO BYI, TRIKE1, Joel Bienz aka TRAP IF, Carlos Mare

I AM ONE WITH THE SUN
RUN WITH THE MOON
WIN WITH THE WIND
DRAIN WITH THE RAIN
I AM THE SOUL OF A SPORT
THRIVE ON ASPHALT
HEAD-TO-TOE DIRTY
THERE IS NOTHING PRETTY ABOUT ME
EVEN WHEN I'M EMPTY
I AM ALIVE
I AM THE WELL, THE PIT, THE HOLE, THE CAGE
I RUN EVERY BOROUGH, AND OWN THIS TOWN
I AM THE PARK PICKUP PLAYER
NO COACH CAN TAKE ME OUT
OR CUT ME BEFORE THE SEASON STARTS
THERE IS NO SEASON
I AM FOREVER ELIGIBLE
I AM FREE

Lettering: Suce (fka Sucio Smash), TRIKE1